Swinsbeck

The story of the Slaters of Swinsbeck

David Barrow

ryelands

First published in Great Britain in 2009

Copyright © David Barrow 2009

All rights reserved. No part of this publication may be reproduced, stored in a retrieval system, or transmitted in any form or by any means without the prior permission of the copyright holder.

British Library Cataloguing-in-Publication Data
A CIP record for this title is available from the British Library

ISBN 978 1 906551 16 2

RYELANDS
Halsgrove House,
Ryelands Industrial Estate,
Bagley Road, Wellington, Somerset TA21 9PZ
Tel: 01823 653777   Fax: 01823 216796
email: sales@halsgrove.com

Part of the Halsgrove group of companies.
Information on all Halsgrove titles is available at: www.halsgrove.com

Printed and bound by Short Run Press, Exeter

CONTENTS

Thanks and Dedication 5

Devon, England 1848 6

Into America 1882 41

New York and West November 1882 65

Chicago and the Stock Yards 78

The Birth of Flight 1905 111

Back to England 1942 132

Swinsbeck 166

Epilogue 190

To those that live in the Blackdown Hills, Devon, or come to that in the USA, you may feel that parts of this story take place in a location you are familiar with.

Swinsbeck is a hamlet purely from my imagination, as are all the characters who in no way represent any persons, living or dead.

THANKS AND DEDICATION

Oh gosh! There are so many people who in some way have been involved in the writing of this story.

Some, like Mary, my wife, and Jutta Irvine who have spent endless hours correcting my spelling, grammar, and generally editing the text. Allan MacDougal, for once again producing a superb cover illustration.

Then there are the numerous friends and family who over the last few months have encouraged me to actually get on and finish. Those, who I cannot name, who made it possible for that to happen.

Most importantly there is you the reader; thank you for buying this book. I hope you enjoy reading it as much as I have enjoyed writing it.

David Barrow
July 2009

DEVON, ENGLAND 1848

1

The southwest wind gusted in with a cruel cold edge to it, flailing the branches of the big beech trees and blowing the last of the leaves away in a cloud of gold.

It had been a wonderful summer, long hot days had come just right for the haymaking in July followed by a few wet days that had been sufficient to fill the grain ready for harvest in August. Now, as the days shortened in the middle of October, the first autumnal gale swept in to rattle the branches and to shake the leaves free as the trees prepared themselves for their winter sleep.

Stephen pulled the old sack tighter round his shoulders and shivered involuntarily when another gust swept in as he stepped out of the back doorway of the farm.

The wind had continued to rise since he had gone out this morning, long before first light, to bring the cows in for milking. Now here he was in late afternoon going to bring them in again, from where they were sheltered in the lea of the far hedge. Not that it gave them much shelter on this flat plateau 600 feet above sea level with nothing between it and the sea twenty miles or so away.

Down in the vale they reckoned that you needed an extra overcoat to survive up here in winter; but then they were a soft lot down there, up here was for real men. Mind you he wouldn't want to go into an inn down there and say that. They might be soft but they were short tempered as well, and had hard fists.

Stephen glanced up at the scudding clouds.

"I better get a move on, there's rain coming in ere long, and heavy at that," he said to himself. "Josie won't want to come out later with this weather blowing up."

ONE

He and Josie had been courting now for two years, having grown up together in Swinsbeck.

She was the third daughter of Judy and Sid Rush the village blacksmith. Stephen had never taken a lot of notice of her until three years ago when she suddenly seemed to mature from a gangling girl into an attractive young woman overnight. She was not classically beautiful, but standing at 5 foot 7 inches, with an hourglass waist (accentuated by the flair of her full long skirt) and small breasts, her long blonde below-shoulder length hair framing a rather too narrow face. She was a good match for Stephen. He was broad shouldered from years of back-breaking farm work, his shock of ginger-coloured hair topped his head at over 6 foot. His face, already weather beaten and ruddy, always crinkling into a cheeky smile hovering round the lips.

Two years ago he had realised that at the great age of 25 it was time that he took a wife, and there was Josie right on his 'doorstep' who certainly took his eye. A prettier filly (and looked like a good breeder too) he would be unlikely to find this side of Exeter.

The next week when he was down at the smithy with old Tug, the great Shire gelding, while Sid had one of the enormous feathered feet clasped firmly into his thick leather apron, between his knees, his back bent double, with smoke drifting up from the sizzling red hot shoe he was fitting, Stephen judged it a good moment to broach the question, while Sid had his hands full as it were. Sid was on the third hoof by the time Stephen had plucked up the courage to speak.

"Your young maid, Josie, is growing up fast," he commented.

"Ugh," grunted Sid, as he plunged the shoe into water to cool it before fitting it to the plate-sized foot.

He was never a man of many words, and the smoke was in his eyes. Anyway, he could not answer while he had a mouth full of nails.

"She must be all of 18 now," Stephen said after a long pause, in fact knowing perfectly well her age.

"I expect she is all of that."

Another long pause, while he swiftly tapped the nails firmly home and wrung off the ends.

"Why do you ask? Sid said as he dropped Tug's foot and walked back to the hearth to heat another shoe, the last.

"I wondered if I might walk out with her?" Stephen asked hesitantly. Sid was a big man and renowned for his quick temper. Stephen was not sure how he would take this request. He had heard that Sid was very protective of his daughters.

Sid poked away at the fire for a minute and gave the foot bellows several lusty stamps which sent the sparks flying upwards into the black cobweb-covered rafters. He bent down to select another shoe from the pile at his feet. He picked up several, but with a quick glance discarded them back to the pile with a ringing clatter, eventually finding one that took his fancy, though for the life of him Stephen could see no difference to the others. Sid plunged it into the brightly glowing coals, poking and raking them around until it was completely covered to his satisfaction.

"Come round after tea on Sunday."

Silence then ensued while he completed the final foot.

I hope Josie has more conversation, thought Stephen as he sat sideways on the broad-backed Tug, who strode deceptively quickly back up the lane to the farm.

This was now three years ago. After that first meeting they had walked out regularly, and his courtship of the girl had blossomed with only periodic disagreements and flashes of temper which Josie had inherited from her father. Initially the attraction had been purely of two young people. This had gradually developed into a deep affection for each other, and finally love.

She had risen from scullery girl to be the personal maid of Mrs Barraclough at the Grange. This was the 'big house' of Swinsbeck. Mr Barraclough was the squire and landowner. An irascible elderly gentleman, who suffered badly from gout, so Josie had told Stephen. He was also now Stephen's landlord, though he had yet to speak to him; payment of rent and any other business dealings were always done through his agent.

Swinsbeck sat on the plateau edge of the hills known as the Blackdowns; 20 miles to the north east of the county town of Exeter. It had been a village site for Iron Age people as the earthworks showed to the western side of the village. Now, other than the blacksmith and St Mark's church, it could only boast of Mrs Caundle's small shop, the Royal George public house, the school and thirty or so cottages lining the one street. Stephen's Cogwell Barton Farm lay half a mile from the village centre while three other farms surrounded the village. The whole lot comprising the Swinsbeck Estate.

Stephen's father had died a year ago last March and the tenancy was now in Stephen's name. He was the only surviving child of four, the others having died at an early age of diphtheria or consumption.

He and his mother lived in the big two-storey thatched farmhouse with its lime-washed cob walls. The dairy and various other storage rooms were part of the house and were joined to the stable. The 'linhay' with the cow-stalls underneath and the pigpens were opposite, a large tithe barn formed the third side of the large cobbled yard, entered by a high archway from the hedge-lined lane that led down to the village. Stephen had been born in the main bedroom upstairs, and his father before him. For all Stephen knew, probably generations of Slaters

ONE

before that. He was not very interested in the past. His life revolved around the changing seasons, the trials and tribulations and the good times of farming.

Josie and he were to be married in the spring. Lambing would be finished and haymaking a couple of months away. Things like marriage had to be fitted in to be convenient for the seasons of the year. Nature wouldn't wait for any man.

They might even manage the journey to Exeter for a night. Josie had never been as far as Exeter so the shops and like would be a real treat for her. That's if Mrs B. would give her the time off. Josie said she was a kindly soul so it would probably be all right.

Stephen pulled the sack tighter over his smock as the first drops of rain were driven in his face by the buffeting wind. Spring could not come too soon as far as Stephen was concerned, though it was a long way off at this time of the year. Spring came late up here. It was always an overcoat colder up on the Blackdowns than in the valleys below.

Apart from the fact he was to be wed, he loved the freshness of spring. A new beginning with first the sudden appearance of snowdrops popping up unexpectedly as from nowhere. Then primroses peeping through the old leaves; later the stitchwort and blackthorn giving a blizzard of white in the hedgerows, and later still the competition between bluebells and wild garlic in the woodlands giving a patchwork of blue and white. Going out of a morning was a real pleasure with the bird song and the dew on the meadows, larks singing as if to burst, the fresh new green leaves as the trees clothed themselves with a new set of finery. None of this cold wet driving rain. How he hated this bit of winter, it seemed to drag on for ever. Though there were the advantages as well; like going in of an evening to a blazing fire in the hearth, the cows inside warm and dry, Christmas with its jollity, and even the beauty of a hard hoarfrost or heavy snowfall. Every season had its special days when he could easily have just stood and looked and listened, breathing in the stillness and beauty of Nature. All in all it was a good life and he wouldn't change it for any other.

He mused to himself as he hurried across to the far hedge. This would never do, there is always work to be done.

"Why are the cows always at the far end of the field when it's raining and won't move to my call?" he thought crossly.

"It will be nice in a month's time when they come into the byre for the winter. I enjoy getting up early on a frosty morning, going into the byre to the lovely warm sweet smell of hay and contented cows, to be welcomed by a soft lowing call. On second thoughts when I am wed it will be better to stay snuggled up to warm Josie Rush. Cor, she's a bit of all right and no mistake. She were like a wild cat, back along."

His thoughts went back to mid-September after the Harvest Supper when he had at last persuaded Josie that they could enjoy now what they would be enjoying on their wedding night. They had both drunk well of the cider provided with the supper, otherwise Josie would never have agreed to accompany him into the meadow. He had not set out or expected that things would turn out like they had, but it had all just gone on from one thing to another. It had started with him putting his arm round her shoulders, and she had responded by snuggling in closer to him with an arm round his waist. Somehow he found his hand creeping down to her lightly rounded buttocks. She had not objected as he turned her to face him closely and they kissed. A long lingering kiss; noses pressed side by side, her small tongue darting in and out of his mouth like a snake's forked tongue. Stephen's left hand now found itself covering her breast which had caused a sharp intake of breath from her. He could feel the taught firmness through her bodice and her nipple hardening as he gently massaged it. She pressed her body hard into his and she could feel the stiffness of his manhood through his breeches. His hands dropped to her hips and were then fumbling with her skirts and petticoats as they tumbled onto the grass; she in her turn was at his breeches like a terrier after a rat.

My goodness, he thought, it had been good. Just the thought of it aroused him again.

The next evening when they had met had not been so good. The cider effect had gone. He could see it coming before she even spoke. She came striding up to him with her blond hair flying over her face in the wind, trying hard to push it to one side.

"Stephen Slater, you took advantage of me in the meadow last evening when you knew I was weak with cider," she stormed at him.

"You had no right to take what was not yours before we are wed."

"I seem to remember that you were a willing partner," he parried.

"Anyways it was bloody good, you must admit." His cheeky broad smile spread slowly across his face.

Josie could not keep her anger going in the face of such an infectious smile. "Yes, it was and all." And they both burst out laughing as they came into each other's arms.

"But you are not going to catch me like that again. We will wait until our wedding night. You will just have to be patient!" she said as she leant back in his strong arms with an impish smile.

"And keep your hands to yourself. Don't start that again."

"That's alright for you to say, but can you wait?" he teased.

Now he supposed he would have to wait, he would never persuade her again like that. However much she had enjoyed it as well, she was a determined young lady who once she had set her mind to something she stuck to it.

The cows reluctantly came out of the lee of the hedge, but then moved quickly away across to the byre into their allotted places. They stood quietly pulling at the hay in the rack in front of them while he fixed their neck chains. Stephen took his stool from the wall and settled down with his head tucked into Buttercup's flank and the bucket between his knees. She was a real quiet one, not like Petal who was a fidget and not averse to trying to kick the bucket across the shed. Soon the steady continuous hiss of the streams of milk flooding into the bucket lulled him into deep thoughts again, as his strong hands gently squeezed the warm teats. He had been milking from the moment he had been able to hold the pail between his knees. It was as easy as breathing to him, and required no conscious thought. His hands just worked away of their own accord; maybe it was the sweet smell of warm cow that lulled his brain. He breathed in deeply.

"How are mother and Josie going to get on when they are living under the same roof? They are both strong-willed women. Of course Rosie will be up at the Grange much of the time, so mother can still feel she is boss in what has been her home for many years. Then there will be the little ones coming along quickly. I am going to enjoy that."

…Thinking back to that September evening again…

Milking at each end of the day was a job he really enjoyed. A good time for reflection, thinking of the tasks that had to be done, and in the evening a good winding down time from the hard physical work of the day; satisfaction at the jobs completed or the new life brought into the world by a successful calving or lambing.

Finished, he turned the cows out into what was now heavy rain sweeping in horizontally across the field. They hurried across the meadow over towards the same hedge Stephen had driven them reluctantly from before milking. He brushed the gutters clean and carried the last milk pail through to the dairy. There was no need to put it over the cooler as his mother would add tomorrow morning's milk to it and start making the cheese for which the farm was well known. He ran quickly across the yard and into the warmth of the old house.

There had been a farm at Cogwell Barton for many centuries. The present farmhouse dated back to the middle of the last century to replace the previous Barton, which had been burnt to the ground one January night when a chimney fire set alight to the thatch. The farm extended to nearly 200 acres, a big farm for the area. As well as the 12 milking cows and their young, Stephen ran a flock of 50 or so sheep, a few pigs and grew 30 or 40 acres of corn. The farm was self-supporting and Stephen was helped by old Cyril who had worked on the farm all his life, other than the six years he had spent in the navy as a pressed boy seaman until he lost his left hand at Trafalgar. Stephen had never discovered exactly how it had happened, although as a small boy he had listened rapturously to Cyril's lurid tales.

Cyril was also the estate 'warrener'; a tradition that had been handed down through his family from generation to generation seemingly from the middle ages. Possibly the Lord of the Manor had given the title to Cyril's ancestors in recognition of loyal service. The title still allowed Cyril to take and to sell as many rabbits from the estate as he wished, though these days Cyril only took what he required and a few to supplement his poor wages. Farm labourers were not the best paid in the countryside.

At haymaking and harvest the itinerant mowing gangs came in, but the rest of the time they managed on their own. Since Father died it had not been easy.

As he entered the kitchen he was greeted by the delicious smell of fresh-baked bread. On the table along with the bread, mother had set a dish of bright yellow butter, a large fatty ham and a great wedge of cheese, with a jug of milk to wash it all down. Next to the gleaming blackened range, in the inglenook, hung more hams, well cured from hanging from the hooks up the chimney in the wood smoke for six months.

They ate their main meal of the day at noon when old Cyril would join them.

Stephen pulled off his dirty wet smock and unlaced his muddy work boots. He went to the sink to wash his face and hands. Not many houses had piped water to the sink. Most would have to carry water from the well to the house.

Father had installed the hand pump at the well a couple of years ago now. It was Cyril's first job of the day to pump the tank in the roof full each morning. This on a normal day would take about a half-hour of nearly 200 strokes unless it was Sunday morning after bath night or Tuesday after washday, when the copper would have been filled to heat a large quantity of hot water. On bath night the old tin bath was brought in; placed in front of the kitchen range, as it had been for as far back as Stephen could remember, and his mother still scrubbed his back as she had when he was a boy, vigorously as if she was trying to rub the skin off. Water was piped to the dairy next door as well which made the butter and cheese-making so much easier.

He pulled on a clean shirt from the drawers in his room before joining his mother at the table. He said grace, as the man of the house. It had seemed strange after Father died (suddenly out in the Long Meadow one afternoon) to take his chair at the head of the table, to say grace and make the decisions.

Father had always been there and he missed him, in spite of the beltings he had received as a boy and the arguments they had had occasionally when he became too strong to be given a thrashing.

ONE

Thinking back once again to his thoughts while milking. They had discussed this before but it was still on his mind.

"Would you rather, when I am wed, that Josie and I should have a couple of rooms to ourselves? I could make the old store by the back stairs into a kitchen with a range and sink."

"No, son, you know we have been over this many times. It will be much easier if we all live together in here. Anyway I want the company now Father has left us. God rest his soul."

"It has been your home for 40 odd years."

"It has been your home for nigh on 27 years too, and will be for many more with Josie your wife and perhaps, God willing, some little ones. Now I will hear no more of it."

The meal over, Stephen pulled on his topcoat and walked on down the village. Although it was pitch black, he had made this journey many times and knew every stone and hole in the road. Anyway there was a glimmer of star shine now when the scudding clouds parted. The rain had stopped for the time being at least but the wind blew as strongly as earlier, and was still roaring in the beech trees, but was veering round into the northwest and definitely had a winter chill to it. He pushed open the door of the Royal George into the smoke-filled warmth of the snug. The blazing fire in the hearth was most welcoming. As usual, Cyril and Stanley Jones occupied their customary seats to either side of the fire, nursing their pitchers of cider that they would make last for the whole evening, unless someone happened to offer them a refill when they would be empty in a trice.

"Evenin' Ernest, Cyril, Stanley. My usual if you will. Rough ol' night."

"It is to be sure... More rain to come I reckon... Did you hear tell of the rick fire out Tiverton way? They say two ricks of wheat and one of oats were lost. You know Dave the carter, he was through here today and the miller told him down at Sheepwash... What's his name?... Oh I just forget now."

"Is that so."

The conversation, such as it was, lapsed and they all continued to gaze into their cider.

2

Swinsbeck was nowhere near the main coach road or centres of news, so local gossip was usually all that filtered through to the village until well after any event had happened.

Stephen looked up to the quietly ticking clock over the bar.

"Josie should be about home by now," he thought.

He drank up the last of his cider, a very rough brew made by Ernest at the back of the Royal George. There had been a time a few years ago when his father had made some of the best cider for miles around from the old orchard behind the Barton. That had all stopped when mother had become sick of father indulging to excess and forbade cider-making on the farm. From time to time in the summer she would find him asleep in the middle of the afternoon under a hedge with a flagon still clutched in his hand.

"Night all."

As he got to his feet the door flew open and a shock of blond hair, blown all ways over her face by the wind, peered round the edge. They all automatically turned to see who was coming in, for a moment Stephen could not see who it was, but that was short-lived.

"I thought I would find you in here, you drunken slob," the apparition pronounced, looking at Stephen.

This sounded like the Rush temper at its worst.

Ernest laughed from the bottom of his stomach. "You've picked a right one there, Stephen Slater. What will she be like when you'm wed? You better get out there quick and get your beating."

He burst into cackles of laughter again, joined by Cyril and Stanley. Stephen ignored Ernest's banter.

"Hello to you too, Josie my love," Stephen said, at the same time glaring at Ernest.

"Don't you 'my love' me. You just come on out here like a man and hear what I have to tell you, as Ernest so rightly says."

He deemed it wisest to do as he was told on this occasion, seeing they were in public and knowing the whole incident would be reported round the village by daybreak.

He went to put his arm round her as the door shut behind them, but was pushed away as Josie headed off up the street at a gallop, holding firmly to his coat, dragging him behind her.

After twenty yards she stopped suddenly, turned, and put her hand on his chest.

"Do you realise what you have done to me?" she shouted. "Your little bit of fun in the meadow has got me with child."

Now both hands were beating hard on his chest and he had just time to wonder where they might move to next, as he stepped hurriedly back a pace.

"What is Father going to say?" she wailed as the tears began to run down her cheeks.

Indeed, what is Sid going to say, Stephen thought… More to the point, what is he going to do?

"Calm down, girl." He held her away at arms length, as much to protect himself as to quieten her.

"Hush now, we don't want the whole county to know. Anyway we had decided to have a big family. We are just starting a little early."

She gasped and glared at him. The thought crossed his mind that it had not been a good thing to say, but his voice seemed to calm her a bit, but it was not going to help with her family.

"What's done is done and the sooner we tell your folk the better. We will just have to bring the wedding forward, though for the life of me it will be difficult with the spring sowing and lambing to get over."

This brought on another flood of weeping.

"To Hell with the lambing and whatever! What about me and what people will think. I don't care about the farm."

He realised that his thoughts had not been very tactful and should have been kept to himself at this moment.

As expected Sid Rush was not best pleased, but did not actually become physical. While Judy, his wife, after the initial shock was secretly pleased to be already on the way to a sixth grandchild.

So on a cold mid-December early afternoon (the cows still had to be milked) Stephen waited at the altar steps for Josie to join him. By his side stood John, his cousin, come up from down in the vale, to be his best man. Stephen pulled out his Father's old Hunter watch for the umpteenth time since he had been standing there; realised it was only half a minute since he had last looked and pushed it back into his waistcoat pocket. He could not stand much more of this; all dressed up like a cockerel, and his collar was far too tight and he was sweating hard in spite of the tomb-like temperature of the church.

"Eh! Do you reckon she's going to show then, Stephen?" asked John in a loud whisper, giving him a sharp dig in the ribs with his elbow.

"Ha, ha! That's a good un ... Going to show, ... eh! ... I can see she is beginning to show all right. When did you manage to catch her?"

The vicar standing in front of them gave John a disapproving look.

"Hold your tongue, young John. This is not the place to make those sort of remarks."

His face took on an even more puce colour than it normally was. He was not averse to a drop or two of gin.

John turned to wink at Josie's younger sister sitting in the front pew. As he did so the church door flew open and a gale of cold air came in, followed by Josie on her father's arm.

Stephen got another dig in the ribs as he turned.

"Get a look at that then" John said in an even louder whisper. "She does look a bit of alright Stephen, my boy. You done all right there."

Indeed Josie did look 'a bit of alright' Stephen had to agree. Her height was emphasised by her blonde hair piled on top of her head and barely covered by the flimsiest of veils. Certainly she was not looking as slim as she had but one would be hard pressed to tell her condition.

She glided up the aisle to stand at his left. Now he could see that her veil was his mother's, that she had worn for her wedding made by Stephen's grandmother many years ago. Granny had been one of the many girls in the area who had learnt the trade of making the hand-stitched fine net and lace, known as Honiton lace, which was so sought after by the rich ladies of London Town.

Stephen's heart nearly burst as he turned to her and received a dazzling smile. He came back down to earth pretty quickly when he caught the glare which Sid gave him. As much to say, 'She's not yours yet, in spite of what you have done to her and my family reputation.'

His father-in-law was never going to allow him to forget that indiscretion.

The ceremony passed in a daze for Stephen until he was brought to his senses by the vicar's words:

"I now pronounce you man and wife. You may kiss the bride."

So Stephen and Josie were wed in The Year of Our Lord Eighteen Fifty-One.

The months went by; spring sowing, lambing, and the first hoeing of the mangles, passing in the usual way.

One evening with a thunderstorm rolling around to the west, down Exeter

| TWO

way, with the mowers booked to come next week to mow off Great Meadow, Stephen turned the cows away to the orchard and plodded his weary way indoors.

"Best watch the milk does not sour too quick," his mother reminded him.

"Thunder can soon spoil it. I reckon we will catch a storm later, hot weather is always followed by a break down to rain."

Josie, who by now looked fit to pop and was finding the carrying of the child a real burden in the close heat of this summer, added:

"I feel it will come later and all. I think my time is coming soon as well; I will be more than glad to get rid of this lump. Stephen, my lad, you have a lot to answer for, it would teach you a lesson if you had to carry this around for a while. I just feels different somehow," she announced, having eaten a hearty tea.

"It will be a good job when you have dropped it. I hope it is not twins. It looks by the size of you that it could be, and you eat enough to feed four at least," Stephen ribbed, "judging by the tea you have just eaten."

"It's alright for you. Here, you have a feel of this that I've got stuck on the front of me all the time."

She placed his large rough hands onto her bulging stomach. He immediately felt the baby move as if in protest.

"Anyway, if it is twins it will all be your fault. You are a lusty lad, that's for certain."

"Oh my! that was a real twinge… Mother, I think it's started" she gasped.

Stephen stepped back with a look of horror on his face, as if he had been responsible for the pang by touching her.

Mother Slater took immediate charge.

"Is that the first pang you have had? You are sure it is not indigestion from tea."

"Yes that was the first, but the babe feels different somehow."

"Stephen, away now down to the midwife. You better call in and tell Judy Rush while you are down there, though God knows, we don't need the whole village up here. No, on second thoughts don't tell her, I could not bear having her fussing around, even if she is Josie's mother."

Stephen, jumping from his chair, where he had returned after the last exchange like a scalded cat, gave Josie a quick careful hug, as if the baby might drop out if he got too close, and was away down the lane at a fast trot.

"Oh, I hope she will be delivered quickly, not like Mary Hutchings who was near two days in labour, and dead at the end of it," he thought, as his breath came in short gasps.

The midwife's cottage was at the far end of the village. Stephen vaulted the low wall round the front of her garden and rapped loudly on the door, which stood open on this hot close evening.

"Mrs," he shouted loudly between breaths as he dashed the perspiration from his brow with his shirtsleeve. In his state of anxiety he could not remember her name for a moment, although he had known her all his life. In fact it was she who had brought him into this world. He rapped again on the door, harder this time. The name came to him as he beat a tattoo on the door.

"Mrs Lutyens, you must come at once."

Mrs Lutyens appeared in the doorway. A short round figure, apron snuggled tightly round her ample middle, her bosom threatening to meet it; Grey hair pushed up untidily under a mop cap, her wrinkled brown face wreathed in a broad smile. She had been the village midwife since, it seemed like, time immemorial. Her age could be anything between fifty and ninety, she probably wouldn't know anyway. She had brought into the world a large proportion of the folks living in the parish.

"Hello, young Stephen. What brings you here in such a rush telling me I must hurry, at this time of day? As if I did not know! Don't tell me. It's that pretty young wife of yours, Josie." She answered herself before he could reply.

"Now have the waters broken?"

"No, not yet, or they hadn't when I left. Mother said to come and fetch you, so I just up and ran."

"I can see that," she replied with a twinkle in her eye.

"Now you just wait a minute while I get my bag for you to carry for me." She disappeared into the dark of the house, emerging a minute later with a shawl draped round her shoulders and carrying an old leather bag, scratched and worn from years of use.

"You take this and give me your arm and help an old lady up the lane."

"We must hurry."

Stephen encouraged her as they plodded slowly through the village with still another half-mile to go, his worry and impatience getting the better of him at the speed of their progress.

Mrs Lutyens came to a halt and turned to him.

"Young Stephen, you have calved or lambed many an animal, and you know very well that birthing does not happen in just a few minutes. An old lady has no need to go any faster just because you say so."

"Well this is different … This is Josie …"

"Well come on, don't stand around gossiping, we must not waste time." She cut him off abruptly, and at the same time cackling with laughter.

She was quite right, there had been no hurry. Josie took another six hours while the thunderstorm drew nearer. In the early morning when the storm broke overhead and the rain fell in a solid mass, Josie was delivered of their first born, a daughter.

They named her Storm. What other name could she have possibly had?

Josie was a loving mother and Mrs Slater a proud grandmother, fussing over the pair constantly and reprimanding Stephen if she felt he was not holding the baby correctly or had not changed his shirt before picking her up.

"Between the pair of you that babe is going to be spoilt rotten, I can tell. What about me, often I have to wait for my meals to be on the table," he chided jokingly.

"Away with you. You have your job to do and we have ours. You are quite capable of looking after yourself but this wee person needs all the attention we can give her," Mrs Slater replied without looking up from where she was cooing over Storm.

The heat of summer turned to the misty days of autumn and Storm grew into a plump contented baby with a head of pale auburn hair the colour of ripe wheat. Stephen had even caught the dour Sid Rush making gurgly noises over her one day.

"She's a fair young maid. My Josie has made a good 'un, but it's what I would expect of her."

Stephen thought it best not to point out that he had played a part in Storm's conception as well. That was something best not mentioned in the presence of his father-in-law, considering the circumstances.

3

The years went by. One season followed another; Storm was followed shortly at regular intervals by two sisters, the second of which succumbed to croup aged six months, much to the distress of Stephen and Josie. This also seemed to drag the will to live from Mrs Slater, who passed away with pneumonia the following January. It was a constantly wet summer with the most difficult harvest that Stephen could recall. Altogether a very bad year that was best forgotten and put behind them. They were a resilient and loving couple and soon another baby was on the way.

At last the longed for son and heir. It had begun to worry Stephen that he wouldn't have someone to carry the family name forward to the next generation and as a successor on the farm. The Slater family had been tenants at Cogwell Barton for a very long time. The tenancy would continue with the Slaters for as long as they wanted it. The landlord had no right to take it away provided the farm was looked after in the way set out in the tenancy agreement.

This son, George (he was named after his paternal grandfather) was always a sickly baby. He never thrived like his older sisters had done, and Josie took many months to get over the birth. The doctor they visited thought that she had worn herself out raising three daughters and now this sickly child, in addition to her duties in the farmhouse and the many tasks she had on the farm. He advised strongly against further children. Stephen could see the sense in this.

Josie was by now a mature woman in her late thirties. She had filled out in stature, not quite the sylph-like figure of well nigh twenty years ago when she had caught Stephen's eye. She was the envy of many a matron and able to turn the heads of the men when dressed up and on a shopping trip to Honiton. When required she was still capable of the 'Rush' quick temper and sharp tongue, but was a devoted mother and wife.

Stephen still liked his drop of cider at the Royal George and Josie, on the odd occasions she partook of something stronger than tea, enjoyed a glass of port. Needless to say after one such an occasion, not quite in the same fashion as years before, the inevitable happened. Harry was conceived, and duly arrived with no trouble or fuss exactly on time.

Right from the start he was a bonny baby, quite different from his elder brother, George. Chubby with bright blue eyes, like his mother and a shock of ginger hair like his father. There was no doubt whose son he was.

George, although only two years older, seemed to resent the new arrival. As they grew up together on the farm his dislike of his younger sibling turned from resentment to initially open bullying, and then deviously laying blame on Harry when he realised that Harry had become more than a match for him.

George was a disappointment to Stephen. His thin frame and weaselly features, reluctance to work at his daily farm chores and lack of interest in anything, including school, tried Stephen's temper to the limit. His belt was only kept from George's backside on many an occasion by Josie's intervention. Stephen was certainly not a violent man but he expected his wishes carried out without question. It was the way he had been brought up and that's how his children should behave. He had had a happy childhood himself and his other three children, if asked, would not have wanted different.

Harry on the other hand was the complete opposite, much like Stephen had been as a young lad. Apart from being the apple of his father's eye, he loved learning at school but was equally happy back home helping with any job, but especially if it involved a piece of farm machinery.

Aged seventeen, George up and left home after another furious row with his father. Josie nearly went out of her mind with worry, and accused Stephen of driving his son away, in spite of knowing in her heart that this was far from the truth. Stephen for his part was deeply saddened that a son of his should have turned out so untrue to form, but inwardly relieved that he was out of the place. This did not stop him making extensive enquiries of George's whereabouts and wellbeing. After two weeks, news came that he had been seen in Exeter in the company of a very rough bunch of young people.

On Josie's insistence, Stephen travelled down to Exeter to try and find him and to encourage him to return home, or at least give him money or set him up with a reliable employer. Find him he did, in a run down rat-infested hovel down near the river; but it only led to another argument with George, quite out of control urged on by his ruffian friends. Stephen left in a seething temper only to over-indulge at an alehouse in the city centre. He found it impossible to understand why George should have a great chip on his shoulder with society and, it seemed, him in particular.

He arrived home the next day very much the worse for wear, a very disappointed man.

Annie, their second surviving daughter was married off to the son of a prosperous shopkeeper from Honiton. She now considered herself rather above the farming family and rarely visited them. Storm, their eldest daughter had left some years before to become a nurse in London, inspired by the stories of the good work done for the poor and sick, that filtered down to the Devon countryside.

Sarah, their next daughter, had always had a much better rapport with George than the rest of the family. It was she who continued to keep a tenuous contact with him and never despaired of getting him to see sense and to give up the vagrant life he had chosen to live, but to no avail. Inevitably he got into trouble with the police for the theft of two loaves of bread and some apples from a small shop down near the river at Exwick. He and his cronies were known in the area and when charged with the crime, George did not deny it.

He was taken to the Borough Gaol to await appearing at the Quarter Sessions in a month's time. It was Sarah, now that she knew where he was, who took him food to supplement the poor diet of bread and potatoes with the occasional bit of mutton floating in a greasy gruel.

The day of the Sessions arrived, with Stephen, Josie, and Sarah sitting in the public gallery. George once again admitted to his misdemeanour when brought before the four worthies of the city sitting on the bench. After a short consultation the chairman pronounced a lenient sentence, as it was a first offence and he had pleaded guilty, of six months' hard labour.

Sarah continued to visit him, and tried to keep his spirits up although she could not change his resolve to continue life at the bottom of the social scale. It seemed to be a self-inflicted hate of himself.

On one such visit, conducted in a small, dark, dank room with a gaoler standing by the door, so no privacy, she resolved to try one last time to persuade him to return home on his release.

He was pushed through the door and abruptly told to sit down at the small table opposite Sarah.

She stretched out her right arm and gripped George's hands, which were folded on the table in front of him. He looked up and his face broke into a faint smile.

"Hello, big sister."

Sarah's heart missed a beat. This was more than she usually got from him. That he should actually greet her before she spoke was a step in the right direction she felt. She went straight to the point, before her resolve weakened.

"George, will you please agree to come home when you are released from this awful place."

| THREE

"We have discussed this before, Sarah, and you know my feelings on the subject," he interrupted crossly. "I know I would not be welcome at home. Father hates the sight of me, Harry is his favourite and he knows it. He cannot do wrong in Father's eyes. No, I must make my own way from now on. I am grateful for the trouble you have taken over me, but that's the way it has got to be."

"No, no, that is not true. Father does not hate you. It is just that you always seem to want to rub each other up the wrong way. You are different, like chalk and cheese, and neither of you will give in to the other. He does of course love you in his own way. Anyway, what about Mother; she loves you and is heartbroken."

George interrupted again: " Then why does she not come and see me in here like you do?"

"Oh George dear, she does love you deeply. She knows that she would just break down in tears to see you in this state. So thin, pale and unkempt. She thinks that it would just upset you as well."

"Just drop the subject, Sarah. You have my answer and that is the end of it. Now tell me about which boy you are courting this week?" he teased.

She thought she would try a different approach to see if she could get through to him how wasteful his life had become.

"Now listen to me, George" she said in a stern voice. A vague smile momentarily brushed across his face. This was a new Sarah to him.

"If you will not come home, will you at least promise me that you will change your way of life? Find some worthwhile job to do and get away from the ruffians you seem to have taken up with. Find a nice girl. Live an ordinary life."

"Look Sarah, I am not making any promises. All I can think of at the moment is to get away from this hell-hole. So please don't go on about it."

His hard labour involved hours spent on the treadmill. A wheel of 24 eight-inch steps turned by the felon continually walking up the steps set on the inside of a wheel. His weight, as he climbed the steps, turned the wheel and the long shaft it was connected to worked the mill, 'beating' straw or hemp to release the fibres for use in rough material. This was used to make mattresses or clothing for the prisoners.

As the months went by George became lean and haggard-looking from his hours spent at this soul-destroying task and the poor diet, in spite of Sarah's food supplementation. Each time Sarah returned more and more distressed at his appearance; and Josie would dissolve into tears having enquired how her boy was faring.

On one such visit Sarah found that George had been released two days before and, in spite of enquiries, she was unable to establish his whereabouts.

She was mortally distressed that he had not heeded her request that he should change his ways.

During these troubled months Harry, or Hal as they called him, had been of enormous support to his parents. He had grown into a strapping lad of fifteen, very like Stephen had been at that age, tall for his years, at 6 foot with a mop of unruly ginger hair. He was already well-muscled and lean, and quite capable of a full day's work in the field (which he had been doing since he was ten) whether it be ploughing behind the team of Shires, or sweating in the summer heat at haymaking or harvest. He had left the village school eighteen months previously and was now an important asset to the farm. However, his one subject of disagreement with Stephen was his love of steam engines and machinery in general. The topic was brought up at regular intervals and invariably ended with one or other stamping from the room. Often as not their conversations on this topic followed the same lines as today:

"Father, did you hear that the Estate down at Broadclyst has got a Fowler engine?"

"Yes, I did that" Stephen replied morosely. He guessed what was coming and continued to look at his account book without glancing up.

"Don't you think we should go down one day to see it?" persisted Hal.

"No, we don't have the time. Anyways I heard tell it had set a rick afire while threshing."

"They are the way farming is going to go in the future for some of the jobs like threshing, ploughing, pumping water, timber pulling and anything that can be driven by belt."

"I said 'No', they are smelly, dangerous, too heavy for the fields, and frighten the cows and horses. I, and Granfer before me, have managed without them so there is no reason why we shouldn't."

This was really quite a long speech for Stephen to make on the subject.

"We have to move with the times and get modern. One could make the argument that we would be better off without wheels on the wagons" Hal said sarcastically.

"That's just plain stupid, now shut up and let a man get on with his work. I won't have them on my farm. Get on out and clean out those pig pens, they are a disgrace."

"I did them this morning. You saw me doing it."

"Don't cheek me. Go, get on with something, Lord knows there's not enough time in a day as it is," and he went grumpily back to his books.

Hal could see that he was not going to budge his father from his long-standing views on how the land should be worked. It was unfair to say the pens were a disgrace, he had seen to them only that morning first thing after he had got the cows in for Father at six o'clock. In truth it was before six as the church had struck the hour as he went across the meadow.

Josie now had a go in her gentle persuasive way, which Stephen had over the years found impossible to hold out against. She had matured from the quick-tempered lassie of twenty-five years ago when she and Stephen had wed. Now she had learnt that it was best to gradually 'drip-feed' ideas to him, and often he would eventually come out with the proposal as if it had been his own.

"Surely it would do no harm to just go down and have a look. The boy works so hard for us and it would be nice if you could give him some encouragement sometimes. I am sure you can spare the time and I could call in and see Old Maggie Borthwick. She has not been right for several months now."

Stephen's head went further down into his books and he just grunted in reply. Josie knew that this was as good as she would get, and usually meant that Stephen agreed and that in the course of time he would make the suggestion as if it had been his idea from the start.

4

It was not to happen, though. George was once again in trouble within a few months of his release from Exeter and disappearance to Lord knows where. This time he had killed a man up in Bristol.

The first they knew of it was when PC Bates cycled up from Honiton. He arrived red in the face and perspiring heavily in his thick buttoned to the neck dark blue serge uniform. Josie greeted him at the door.

"Come in, Constable. My, you look fit to bust. It is a hot afternoon to be sure. Take a seat and I will get you a nice cooling drink. Water or milk, being on duty I imagine, so you would not wish for a glass of cider? Though for the life of me I can't think what brings you here on duty," she said with a twinkle in her eye.

She knew that Constable Robert Bates was not averse to something a bit stronger. She had known him a long time and he had the reputation round the villages that he liked a drop of ale or cider. In fact it was probably the reason he was sent out on calls such as this, to sweat out the previous day's drink. Also quite possibly the reason he had never become sergeant.

"Thank you Missus. I think I will try a glass of your cider. It's a long drag up from town and a man does need some refreshment, and as you says it's a mighty hot day even for this time of year. I have come on police business, and I think I should talk to the master. It's about your young George."

Josie blanched, set the glass down with a bump, slopping the amber liquid over the side. She hurried to the door and across the yard to where Hal was busy fitting new shares to the plough.

"Hal, my love, away quickly to find your father. Tell him Constable Bates is here to see him. It's important and he must come quickly."

"What's up Mother? The steers been out again into the squire's garden?" he joked.

"Off with you now" she scolded him crossly.

Stephen strode in a few minutes later.

| FOUR

"Hello Constable. Ah, that's good, I see Josie has given you something to whet your whistle. I will have one too, please, my love. Now what brings you all the way up here, Constable? It's a tidy push up the hill for one of your age" he said without pause, and without noticing the expression of consternation on Josie's face.

"Ugh, it's your young George, Sir."

"What's he been up to this time? Got hi'self into another scrape I don't doubt" Stephen joked, but knowing inside that it was more trouble.

"Rather more than that, I fear, this time, Sir." He paused and took a long draught of the amber liquid.

"Come on then, man. Out with it," Stephen interrupted, a worried expression clouding his face suddenly.

"He has killed a man up in Bristol, we are told," the Constable replied in a rush.

Stephen looked up sharply, his glass half raised to his mouth. Josie sat down heavily in the nearest chair, her hand to her mouth stifling the gasp as the awful truth hit her.

"My boy killed a man. It could not be. What happened?"

"I fear it is true, Sir. Apparently he got into a drunken brawl with this man over some woman, pulled a knife and stabbed him right through the heart. It was in an inn near the docks with many witnesses to the crime."

"Where is he now?" Stephen's face had gone as red as the constable's with his anger and consternation at this news.

"At present he is still up at Bristol, but we are told he is to be transferred to Exeter, as he is a Devon lad, once he has appeared before the magistrates. He will go to the County Prison at Northernhay to await the next Assizes. This is all I can tell you at present. I am sorry to be the bringer of such bad news. Now I must get on back to the Station."

He drank up the rest of his cider in one long draught and hurried away, his face nearly as red with embarrassment as when he had first puffed in, only too pleased to get away having finished his unpleasant duty.

The next day Stephen and Josie travelled to Exeter to find a lawyer to handle the case for them. They had hardly spoken since the shattering news. Josie had dissolved into floods of tears, with Sarah nearly as bad. Stephen had gone about his work with a long face and looking like thunder; impossible to tell what his thoughts were, snapping at Hal about the most petty of things. Eventually Hal resolved to just try and keep out of his way and to get on with the work as best he could.

The visit to the lawyer achieved nothing other than that he would represent George at the Assizes, having found out the evidence of the case. He would be in touch with Stephen when George had been transferred to Exeter, assuming that the case would be heard there. He was not encouraging and, when asked, stated what Stephen already suspected: that if found guilty of murder the penalty was death.

After ten days he wrote to Stephen saying George would be transferred the following week and giving more details of what had happened. There was not much of a case on which to defend him. He had not been particularly liked in the pub or the part of Bristol he had lived in; he obviously behaved to all people in the manner that he had at home, so there was nobody to give him a 'character' reference. Witnesses to the stabbing, though reluctant to help the police, were not hard to find.

The Crown's case was soon put together and the trial set to come up at the Western Circuit Summer Assizes towards the end of May.

The day before the trial was due to start, Stephen, Josie, and Sarah travelled to Exeter and put up at an hotel near the centre of the city and not far from the Castle at Northernhay where the trial would take place in the Crown Court. Hal had to stay back at the farm to mind the stock. He was disappointed not to be able to go and support his brother in spite of their past differences.

The appointed day arrived. The family were early to court to try and avoid the crowds of public and newsmen. The trial had generated great interest locally; people seemed to have a morbid interest in anything gruesome; it was probably a carry-over from the days of public execution the last of which, at Exeter, had been only ten years before, when Mary Ashford had been hanged for poisoning her husband. The crowds had gathered early to watch, lining the slopes of the Long Brook valley to get the best view.

George's trial was before Mr Justice Humphreys, an ominous name from the past, but apparently not in any way related. George was brought up from the cells flanked by two warders. He looked haggard for his years, his hair long and unkempt, but his clothes clean and well pressed. This was due to the love and care Josie and Sarah still felt for him; they had brought a well washed and ironed old suit and shirt from home, and arranged for it to be delivered to the prison. He still presented a sorry sight.

Stephen's thoughts were mixed, as he sat with the others. He could not condone the taking of another life, if that is what the court decided, but George was still his son and in his own way he loved him as deeply as any of his other children. Though, Lord knows, it had been a hard task at times. He just could not understand how a son of his could have turned out in such a way. What had he done wrong in George's upbringing that had led to this situation? Should he have treated him differently from the others? Given in to his peculiar ways and tantrums? Been more open with his love for this mixed up child? It was not his way though; in hindsight he should have tried harder, he accused himself.

The trial followed a normal course. A jury of twelve worthy citizens were sworn in, with no objections from either the defence or Crown. George was asked to confirm his name, which he did in a subdued whisper without even looking up.

"Speak up, boy. Everybody needs to hear what you say. If you just mumble it does you no good," Mr Justice Humphreys leaning forward addressed George.

The Crown made their case. They called the police officers that had made the arrest and investigated the crime; witnesses from the scene, most of which were vague in their evidence and many of whom did not recognise the short-bladed knife found still clutched in George's hand when arrested; the doctor who had attended the scene, and the pathologist who confirmed that the victim had died of a stab to the heart. The girl who had been the centre of the dispute was just glad to be the centre of attention, and would have said anything to achieve this. She was obviously a street prostitute with a painted face and barely concealed bosom; Stephen hardly dared look towards her, let alone catch her eye; The defence lawyer hired by Stephen cross-examined all these witnesses but without really producing anything new that might have swung the jury in favour of George.

The day ended with a cloud of depression hanging over the family as they threaded their way back to the hotel through the news reporters trying hard to get a quote from them. Stephen was hard-pressed to keep his temper and it was only the fact of having his wife and daughter on his arms that kept him from lashing out. The women both dissolved into another flood of tears on arrival back in their room. This was just too much for Stephen who took himself off to the bar where he sat all evening talking to no one and becoming more and more inebriated, as the evening went by, until he was turned out when the bar closed.

The following day a very hung-over Stephen and the women sat morosely behind the defence lawyer's team while they tried to make a case on his behalf. Their doctor and vicar from the village were called to try and establish a character for him, but really there was little that could be said to help. The Crown and Defence made their closing statements and Mr Justice Humphreys summed up before the jury were dismissed to consider their verdict. They were not out for long before returning.

They unanimously found George guilty of murder.

The Court then rose for the day and for the Judge to consider the sentence. He would rule on this the next morning.

"What hope have we got?" asked Stephen of their lawyer.

"Very little, I fear. There are only two alternatives he can consider: Life imprisonment, or the death penalty. Mr Humphreys is thought to be a fair judge, but in the past has ruled both ways, so I can't guess the outcome."

"What about deportation to one of the penal colonies? Though I feel that could be just as bad," asked Sarah.

"No. That is not a possibility, I am afraid, my dear. Deportation was stopped some years ago. The colonies got tired of having all our criminals lumped upon them. I can't say I blame them either. We will appeal, of course, if the verdict goes against us. You must not raise your hopes that it might be successful though. We really do not have any case, as you have heard."

Stephen resolved not to repeat his excesses of the previous evening, and they all sat for the evening together, each in their own deep thoughts, only picking at supper in spite of not having eaten all day.

The family reluctantly took their seats in court next morning, silently praying for a lenient verdict. The court usher brought their attention back to earth.

"The court will rise." Mr Justice Humphreys took his seat having nodded his acknowledgement.

"I have carefully considered all the evidence put before me." He paused. "Please all stand while I pass sentence."

George stood impassively. Staring straight ahead; his gaze seeming to be oblivious to his surroundings and everybody about him. He did not once look towards the family. Sarah found this particularly sad and had difficulty in controlling her sobs.

Mr Humphreys reached below his desk and withdrew his black cap. There was a gasp from the floor of the court.

Josie covered her face with her hands and sank slowly back on to the bench; head bowed to her knees. Stephen's arm went round her shoulders, as much to give comfort to himself as to Josie.

"George Slater, you have been found guilty of this heinous crime. You will be taken from this place and on the appointed day shall be hanged by the neck until you are dead."

On hearing these words George turned his head and looked down from the dock to where the family were sitting. A smile briefly crossed his face before turning away again without catching the eye of any of them.

The Court erupted in a babble of noise, with several people, probably the press, rushing for the doorway.

Over this clamour the court usher called for quiet as Mr Justice Humphreys left the bench.

| FOUR

Stephen turned immediately to their lawyer:

"We must get this sentence reduced to, at the least, life imprisonment, though God knows that is as bad. Get the appeal underway. No expense to be spared."

Stephen stumped away, his face like thunder.

"Can we see George before he is taken back to the prison? Please, they must allow this" pleaded Sarah.

"I will see what I can arrange, but it is not normally permitted," replied their lawyer.

"No, I just could not see him at this time," wailed Josie as the tears flowed again.

The lawyer returned after five minutes, still wearing his wig, and with a pleased expression on his face.

"Miss Slater, in the circumstances his honour will allow you just a few moments with your brother."

Sarah was led down to the cells by the bailiff. The stone steps were cold and dank, lit only by one lamp, the little light it gave out 'fluttering' in the draught.

"Mind how you go, Miss. It is easy to trip."

George sat on the bench behind the iron bars of the cell; his head hung to his knees.

Sarah clutched the bars with both hands, her knuckles white with the intensity of her grip.

"George, my dear, have heart, do not lose faith. Dad is getting the appeal going immediately."

George looked up; his eyes deep sunk in the black holes of the eye sockets, his head looking skull-like in the poor light; his air of defiance from the dock had gone; he now looked like the forlorn little boy that she had comforted so often in the past when he had been in trouble at home.

"Sarah, dear, why have you come down here? It is best that you all just forget about me. I must pay the penalty for what I have done, and that's all there is to say."

"Don't say that. Mother was too distraught to come down now, but we all love you. You know that."

"That's not true, and you know it. Dad has never loved me; I have always been a disappointment to him, not like Hal who has lived up to his standards. I never wanted to be a farm labourer which is what he expected of me."

"Oh, that is far from the truth George. He can be a taskmaster at times, I know, but he has tried hard to understand you. The trouble is you are both strong characters but as different as chalk from cheese. He does love you, I know, but sometimes he has trouble in expressing that love in a way that can be understood."

Sarah realised that they had had this conversation, almost word for word, on many previous occasions. She felt frustrated that she was unable to think of any new argument that might convince him.

"Sorry Miss, you must go now, they are ready to move the prisoner back to the prison, said the bailiff.

George got to his feet and came over to the bars, clutching them tightly, his knuckles white, drained of blood by the intensity of his grip, only just holding himself together.

"Thank you for coming, Sarah, my dear. You have always been so good to me. The only one of the family who understands me, but please don't come again."

Sarah was ushered out and up the steps to rejoin Josie.

"How is he?" she asked tearfully.

"He is not well, I am sure. He is just a frightened little boy, Mother; we must win the appeal. It's very distressing to see him, and he said he did not want us to see him again. I think he is resigned to his fate."

She became overcome by tears and had to sit down quickly to avoid fainting. The strain of the last few weeks was taking its toll on all of them. When would this nightmare be over?

Their lawyer sent the appeal up to The Home Office for consideration by the Home Secretary. He, supposedly, passed it on to three learned judges for their perusal to see whether they should recommend a change to the sentence passed out by Mr Humphreys. Sarah would have liked to go up to London to speak to the Home Secretary on George's behalf, but was forbidden by her parents who feared for her safety, unchaperoned in a wicked city which was how they conceived London to be. They had never ventured out of Devon, and the thought of making the long train journey to the 'big city' was too much for them. It would have been quite an undertaking, anyway; first the coach to Exeter, next the train journey, via Bristol, which would take about twelve hours, followed by having to find lodgings in a strange place. Apart from all of that they felt quite unable to face another session of inquisition as the learned gentlemen mulled over the evidence.

"Anyways. Why whould the man be interested in listening to the likes of you? We be just country yokels in the eyes of those lot up there. What good is it going to do, the boy killed a man, the evidence made that quite clear," Stephen replied crossly, leaning forward with his head on his arms on the kitchen table.

"Oh Dad. You can't say that. We must not give up hope."

As everybody had forecast; the news came, on a cold grey December day, that the appeal had been turned down and execution day was set for 28th February.

| FOUR

The family travelled again to Exeter in the middle of February in the hopes that George would agree to see some or all of them, but to no avail. He was quite determined to face the last days of his life alone.

On the 27th February a notice was fixed to the prison doors, giving notification of the execution to be carried out the following day. It did not state a time, but this did not stop Sarah and Rosie arriving at the gates, along with a small crowd, before first light. They knew nobody, and nobody knew them, but both were upset at the sometimes ribald comments passed among the spectators. They were unable to understand why complete strangers should have been drawn to the prison early on a cold morning only to make jokes about the 'Crack neck' as hanging was known. Perhaps still a morbid carry over from the days of public hangings.

George was led from his cell, having refused breakfast, at shortly before nine. He was quite calm in himself having prayed with the chaplain for ten minutes beforehand.

His journey was only up a short flight of stairs and into a room occupied by the County Sheriff, a surgeon, the chaplain and the executioner, who the day before had 'viewed' George in his cell in order to judge his weight. This was important as it determined the drop required on the scaffold to ensure the neck was broken quickly and cleanly; there had been many instances in the past where the neck was not broken and the prisoner died a slow death of strangulation.

The verdict of the court was read out again and signed by the sheriff. George just nodded when asked whether he understood the sentence.

He was blindfolded; his arms tied behind his back, and legs secured together at the ankles by the executioner, who was an unremarkable man in his late fifties, short in stature, bowlegs, thin to the point of looking starved, and thinning grey hair. He placed the knotted rope round George's neck, ensuring the knot was beside his left ear, stepped back and pulled the lever quickly behind where George stood. There was no sound other than the trap doors dropping down.

The chaplain intoned a prayer and followed the sheriff and surgeon out of the door and down to the room below where the surgeon certified the body dead, and the sheriff and surgeon signed to confirm the execution had been completed.

So ended the unnotable and unhappy life of George Slater on a cold February day. The world continued to turn, the people of Devon continued with their lives and the incident was soon forgotten, except by the Slater family whose lives would never be the same again.

The notice of execution was posted on the prison doors, which was the first Josie and Sarah knew that the sentence had been carried out. They were both completely cried-out and in a state of shock, unable to recall what they then did or how and when they returned home. Josie retired to her room and stayed there for over a week, hardly touching the food Sarah tried to persuade her to eat. Stephen could not talk to her and was not in Sarah's good books either.

"Dad, you should have been there to support Mother. I know it has been a traumatic time for all of us, but Mother really needed you at that time."

"No, I couldn't. George had rejected me and blamed me for the position he had got himself into. Mother, although she has not said it, is of the same opinion. I am inclined to agree with them. I should have done more for the boy"

"That is not true, and you know it really. We are all to blame to a certain extent, but it is the way of life he wanted to lead. The way he was made; the way he thought was different to us. He was different, too; he was not cut out to be a farmer like you and Hal, and Mother and me. I don't know what would have been right for him and probably we should all have tried harder to understand him. He is gone now and we must get on with our lives. Not forget him, but perhaps learn something from it."

Stephen took Sarah in a great bear hug of affection.

"Oh, my girl, what a wise speech for someone as young as you. I wish Mother and I were as strong as you have been over the last few months. You were the only one he trusted and who understood him. I was too dogmatic and set in my ways to adapt to him, though he was always a difficult child right from when he first sucked." At last the tears were allowed to flow freely down Stephen's cheeks. He felt humbled by his daughter.

It was now that Sarah and Hal kept the farm going and the running of the house and business ticking over. Stephen took more and more to drinking heavily, while Josie seemed to have lost her interest in life and her appearance, allowing her once lovely hair to become uncombed and dry looking. Sarah, who had been walking out with a farmer's son from down the vale, married him at Swinsbeck village church later that year. It was a happy day but Stephen and Josie were unable to enjoy it, with their long faces, which tended to put a damper on things, not to mention that Stephen had to be escorted home by Hal early at the reception when he started to become abusive through drink. Sarah's departure meant that the atmosphere at Cogwell Barton became ever more morose and difficult. Things went from bad to worse when Josie, who had never really recovered from the drama and shock of George's death, contracted pneumonia early the next year and died within days of the first anniversary of that death, at the early age of forty-eight. Stephen drank more and more heavily and now blamed himself for Josie's death as well as George's. He did not bother to go up to bed at night, instead remaining in his chair in a brandy-soaked stupor. He rarely washed or shaved and only picked at the food put before him by Hal, or the lady who now came in to help from the village. She was always on the point of leaving due to the abuse given to her by Stephen. Hal was for ever having to persuade her to stay after yet another slanging match between them.

Hal had to bear the full responsibility of the farm in which he was not totally interested. He was an avid reader of any leaflets, books, or maintenance manuals of anything mechanical; he was at his happiest when he was able to get his hands on a spanner or able to ride over to watch (or hopefully help) if a steam-engine was in the area. Now, as master of the farm, he hired an engine and team to come and do the corn threshing out of the ricks in winter. The railways were a fascination to him, but he was a home-loving country boy at heart and was a bit fearful of the time and distances that they covered. Anyway, he was very aware of the fact that it was only by his hard work that the farm did not slip into a state of decay which would have meant loss of the tenancy.

Drink, and probably a broken heart, eventually caught up with Stephen eighteen months after Josie died. A good gathering of friends and neighbours assembled at the little church in Swinsbeck, in the middle of July, with Hal and his two sisters. Storm was abroad somewhere doing good works. Stephen had been well liked in the area and regarded as a good progressive farmer for the times, but had become something of a recluse over the last few years. The wake was held at Cogwell Barton, arranged by Sarah and some of the ladies of the village. Annie saw herself as being above that sort of thing, but sent up pies and cakes. She had been ashamed to have been associated with a family who had a son hanged for murder. She had made little effort to visit either her mother or father when they most needed her. This was a great disappointment to Sarah who had been a tower of strength in spite of having a life and family of her own.

5

It was assumed by the Estate that Hal would continue as tenant of Cogwell Barton. Squire Barraclough had been succeeded by his eldest son, a gruff but kindly man who had spent many years away in India in the army. He was sympathetic and helpful to Hal at this difficult time.

Hal was of two minds about his future. He now had no ties at all with the farm, but it was his home and where he had spent all twenty years of his life, never having been out of the county. On the other hand he had this great love of all things mechanical and the developments in this field that he could see for the future.

In the end he decided to take the tenancy and see how things turned out, perhaps he would be able to combine his two passions. At last perhaps Cogwell Barton could feel the strength and power of steam working in the fields on a regular basis, which had been denied during Stephen's time.

His second year as master of Cogwell Barton was a disaster. Most of the cows aborted and milk production virtually stopped, consequently his cheese and butter customers took their business elsewhere. The hay and corn harvests were a wash-out, the wettest summer in living memory. Hal was despondent; the long hours he put in were for nothing.

It set Hal thinking again that there must be openings in another life rather than the drudgery of the one he had at present. He was always working, not that he minded that, but apart from the odd visit to the pub he never had a chance to meet anybody. Farming, in the depths of the countryside, was a very lonely existence. There did not seem to be any girls in the village that caught his eye in the same way that his mother and father had met and fallen in love.

Sarah and he had grown very close in the years since their father had died. They discussed Hal's life, and her own on her husband's family farm; this really set Hal thinking. He had heard that there were great prospects opening up in America. It was a big decision for him to make but he decided to give up the tenancy and emigrate and see what he could make of a completely new life. He was a strong young man with his skills and interest in engineering, so surely there would be openings for him. America, he had read was an emerging country full of opportunity. In such a vast country there must be a place where he could settle and prosper. The second problem that it would solve, if the Squire agreed, would be for Sarah to take on the tenancy of Cogwell Barton with her husband Richard, who was the second son in his family and therefore probably had no hope of inheriting their family farm.

Once he had reached these conclusions he set things in motion immediately. He decided that for the time being he would not mention it to Sarah in case it was not possible, then there would not be any disappointment. The next day, dressed in his best and only suit, he called at the Manor, by appointment.

"Good morning, young Slater. What brings you to see me on such a fine morning? I suppose you are hoping we will reduce your rent after such a bad year."

"No Sir, though that would be nice," Hal said with his infectious smile breaking out over his face. "I have come to give you notice on my tenancy, and to make you a request," he rushed on in one breath.

"Oh, I see. That's a big decision to make, and what is this important request?"

"Well Sir, I know it is unusual, but would you be prepared to pass the tenancy on to my sister Sarah and her husband."

The Tenancy Laws stipulated that the right of succession to a tenancy was passed through the male line and so Sarah had no right to take it on from Hal.

"That, young man, is an unusual request. I am sure you realise that tenancies are only handed down from father to son. I would have to think about this, and take some advice. I know Sarah, but I must know more about her husband. It would be him that would look after Cogwell even if the tenancy was in Sarah's name. As you know well, we are very particular about the careful upkeep and maintenance of our properties," he said, with a twinkle in his eye. They could both recall the fuss there had been a few years back when he had taken one of his tenants to court over a broken agreement.

"I know they live down in the vale with his parents on a small farm. Is he a hard working lad? Yes, I am sure he is or you would not be here. As you well know, Cogwell is a lot for a young man to take on. Once again, all I can say at the moment is that I will make some enquiries of acquaintances that live down that way, and have a good think about it. Come and see me in a week and we can talk some more."

"I have said nothing to my sister about this, Sir. I would be obliged if you could keep any enquiries as discreet as possible."

Hal left, determined that he would give up the farm even if Sarah and Richard were unable to move there in his place. It would be nice if she could move, as it would be continuing the Slater dynasty at Cogwell Barton, even though the name would no longer be the same. It would really give them a foot in the door of farming. That's if things went better for them than they had for him recently.

As ordered, a week later Hal presented himself on the Manor steps, once again polished and spick and span. He was shown into the library and soon joined by the Squire.

"Well then, Hal. Do you really want to give up Cogwell? Have you really thought about it over the last week? It is a big decision to take. What do you plan to do instead? You have to earn enough to keep a crust in your mouth. I would be sorry to see you leave. You have really coped very well the last few years. But then you had a good teacher in your father."

"Yes Sir, my mind is set to emigrate to America and see where my life goes in that great country. There must be work that will suit me. I am very interested in all things mechanical, which I believe is the way forward for agriculture and industry. I read that there are many opportunities over there if one is prepared to work hard."

"A brave decision, my boy. I wish you well. I am sure you will succeed at whatever you set your mind to. I expect you are right about these wretched machines, though I must say I do not like them one bit. Give me a good horse any day. Now to the other little matter you asked about. Your family have always been good tenants both for me and my father before me, and your family through your Mother have had a long association with mine as well. I would be sorry not to have a Slater in the village, even if she is not called by that name. However, as I told you before, it would be breaking a precedent to give the tenancy to a woman. Ask Sarah and her husband to come and see me this coming Friday. I will consider the matter further… What's his name by the way?"

"Richard Watts, Sir. Thank you, Sir."

Late Friday morning, as Hal came across the yard, Sarah came running up in a flurry of petticoats obviously full of excitement.

"It's ours, it's ours," she gasped. "I've run all the way from the Manor, I just had to give you the news as soon as possible. Oh thank you, Hal, so much. It was all your doing and what you must have said to the Squire." She flung her arms round him and hugged him hard, tears running down her face with pleasure.

"Heh, hold on a minute, you are squashing the breath out of me. What on earth are you talking about?" he teased.

| FIVE

"Oh Hal you know perfectly well. The Squire has given us the tenancy of Cogwell. What else could I be so pleased about? Why did you not say something when you told Richard he wanted to see us? You did not tell me you were going to America either. Oh, my dear, what are you going to do there?"

A look of concern crossed her face.

"To be honest I have not the faintest idea at the moment. The first thing is to get there and see what turns up."

It was now Hal's turn to give her a hug, and shake Richard's hand as he walked up.

"Well done both of you. You must have impressed the old man. Come on in and we will drink to many years of happiness for you here. There are also the arrangements we will have to make for the value of the stock; we had best get the valuer in. I must have something to start me in my new life. You did not imagine that I was going to go without being paid to get out, do you?"

"Richard, we must away to the bank in town to arrange a loan." Sarah immediately became the practical businesswoman.

The arrangements were made. Sarah and Richard secured a loan from the bank to enable them to pay off Hal, though he was very generous in the amount he eventually agreed to. Sarah took over the tenancy at Michaelmas. They moved into the Barton, and Hal spent hours with Richard walking from field to field passing on every item of knowledge he had acquired over the years, such as where the wet patches were in fields; the best fields for growing corn, even where the foxes had their earths to which they would take the odd lamb. Hal sorted through his belongings, trying to decide which to take with him. He did not wish to be encumbered with more than a shoulder bag. Those he did not need on his travels but was loath to discard, he left in Sarah's good care.

He planned to travel to Southampton where, he had heard told, he would be able to take passage for America. The day of his departure arrived all too quickly.

Sarah was in floods of tears. Hal had a lump in his throat and his stomach felt as if it had a knot in it from the excitement and worry about the adventure he was about to set out on.

"My little brother, you will be careful, and you must write to me as soon as you are settled somewhere. I want to hear all about America and who you meet, what work you are doing; everything. You promise you will let me know." She embraced him with a motherly hug, in spite of the fact that the top of her head only came to under his chin. She had always been more of a mother to him than a sister.

His adventure was about to begin. He shouldered his bag and set forth for the coach to Exeter to catch the train which would take him to Southampton.

He turned as he walked through the farm gate for one last glimpse of his home of twenty-two years. He was going to miss the old place. His whole life had been spent within a few miles of Cogwell. The steps he was taking were steps into the complete unknown. What would the future bring for him and where would he end up?

The southwest wind gusted in with a cruel edge to it, flailing the branches of the big beech trees and blowing the last of the leaves away in a cloud of gold.

He pulled up his coat collar, turned and strode away without looking back. A tear came to his eye which he brushed impatiently away with the back of his hand.

INTO AMERICA 1882

6

Exeter station was a new experience for Hal. He had been to the city of Exeter on a few occasions but never to the station. He was very familiar with the steam engines that worked round the countryside, and he had seen the trains from a distance as they puffed up the incline through the valley. However, he had never got up close to an engine.

He could not resist hurrying up the platform to inspect the engine, pushing his way between the porters and trolleys loaded with all sorts of luggage, boxes, crates of small animals, milk churns and newspapers. As he approached the engine he was entranced by the 'sleeping' power radiating out from the gleaming monster. He breathed in the nectar of the smell of hot oil and heat as the steam gushed out in a gasping cloud in the cold air. He was enveloped in a fog of damp air for a moment before it evaporated towards the station roof.

The thoughts of Sarah, Cogwell and homesickness that had been in his mind since walking away from the farm, soon disappeared as quickly as the steam from the engine.

The monster shone in the bright sunlight from its polished livery. It seemed to be saying to Hal 'Look at me. This is the start of your new life. I will rush you away on your adventure.'

He was still standing there in something of a trance, admiring the great wheels and connecting rods, when the guard's whistle blew and he had to hurry to take his place in a carriage. This was an exciting start to his journey. He sat with his nose pressed to the window, enjoying every minute as they rattled through the countryside with the smoke from the engine drifting out to the side, blown into shreds in the strong wind. The bumpty bump of the wheels on the track could have been very soporific but he was far too excited to drop off to sleep. As they passed farmers toiling in the fields, like he had done for so many years, he was especially glad he had taken this plunge to start a new life. Everything looked good from where he was sitting, with the decision he had made to start afresh.

To Hal, Southampton seemed very like Exeter. A busy bustling place, everybody rushing hither and thither about their own business. Carts and carriages pushed their way through the people, who seemed to have no time for a lengthy chat or gossip, which was what Hal was used to in the countryside. There was a continual noise from the traffic rumbling over the cobbles and from the shouting shopkeepers and stallholders selling their wares. It was early evening by the time he had found the town centre and he had worked up a good thirst and hunger having only had the lump of bread and cheese given to him by Sarah as he left home.

He went into a large pub and ordered a pint of mild and a helping of meat pie from the young barmaid. She had noticed the handsome red-headed young man as he had walked in the door and had nudged her colleague behind the bar.

"Heh girl, take a look at that just walked in the door, I would not mind a bit of that, eh! Different from the louts we normally have to fight off. Just you look at the shoulders on him."

She brought over Hal's pie to the table where he sat alone.

"Thanks love, smells good. I have a fair hunger on me, I could eat a horse." He looked up and smiled broadly at her.

"Probably is. Where are you from? You don't sound as if you are from these parts, off a ship then?" Tossing her hair and putting one hand on his shoulder, and pressing her thigh against his side, flirting outrageously.

"I've just come up from Devon to take ship to the Americas as soon as I can find a passage. Would you know if I can take a room for the night here?"

Hal was finding her close presence slightly embarrassing. This was not the way girls behaved in Swinsbeck on meeting for the first time. Come to that, he did not have a lot of experience of the opposite sex. He had always been working too hard to have much time for them.

"Yes, they do have rooms, but rather rough. Though a young country boy like you would be used to that sort of thing, I expect. I will go and ask if they have one free."

She was back in a few minutes. "Come with me and I will show you where it is; sixpence a night, all in," she said with a giggle as she turned without waiting for his reply and disappeared through a door at the end of the bar, waggling her backside seductively. Hal quickly drained the last of his beer, grabbed his bag, and followed her through the doorway and up a dark stairway to the second floor. His embarrassment was roused again as she lifted her skirts above her ankles to climb the stairs. He could not help but catch a glimpse of a pretty pale well-rounded leg. He could feel his face turning red as he blushed.

The room was not much bigger than the bed with its thin straw mattress. It all looked not exactly clean, especially the mattress and the worn mat on the floor. He decided that it would do for the night until he could find something else, if he was going to have to wait for a ship. Anyway it was quite cheap. He would have to be careful of what he spent as he did not have unlimited funds. He had been more than generous to Sarah and Richard by not taking as much value from Cogwell as he might have done, but then Sarah had been like a mother to him these last few years, even after she moved away down the vale.

"My room is on the floor above," the barmaid said, glancing sideways at him with half closed eyes and a flick of her head. "Do you want it? Make your mind up. I must back down to the bar. They will be thinking I'm up to no good," she said abruptly with a smile and a twinkle in her eye.

"Yes, it will do. I will come down and have another pint."

The one pint became several more as he sat at the bar talking to the girls in between them serving other customers, who seemed to Hal a friendly lot when he struck up conversation with them. This was a new life for him, but the chatter took his mind off any feelings of homesickness.

Reason overcame his desire to continue the conversations and he took himself off up the stairs to his room. He pulled off his boots, coat and shirt and tumbled onto the mattress, which after only a few minutes seemed to be all lumps as he tossed and turned to get more comfortable. It didn't stop him dropping off to sleep, however, helped no doubt by the ale he had consumed. He vaguely heard the light step as someone went on up the stairs to the floor above; then the beer and excitements of the day overcame him again as he dropped off into a deep sleep.

It seemed only moments later that he was woken by a light knock on his door, and the latch clicking open. He sat up in bed, startled out of his deep sleep. Before he could speak to enquire who was there he was addressed in a loud whisper:

"Are you awake?" He recognised the voice of the barmaid.

"Yes, what do you want?"

"A girl gets quite cold these nights up under the roof on a winter's night. I thought that perhaps you could warm a girl up a bit." The door latch clicked again and she crept to his side and pulled his blanket back to slip in along with him on the narrow mattress.

Hal was lost for words. This had certainly never happened to him before; in fact he had never been as close to a girl wearing what felt like only a thin shift.

He could feel all too well many soft bits pressing against him. There was no room to draw away as his back was pressed hard against the wall, and the narrow bed did not allow for anything other than very close contact. Anyway he was becoming quite certain that he did not wish to move, especially as her hands began to move over his body and he became fully aroused. He had always been a quick learner and was soon responding in a similar way discovering things he had never known existed.

"I have never done this before," he admitted sheepishly.

"Yes, I can tell that, but never mind I like what you are doing. I thought it all just came naturally to you country boys."

Later he woke to find himself alone on the bed. He thought that if this was the way his new life was going to unfold then it was not half bad, as he dropped off to sleep again.

Hal woke early as he was accustomed. His first thought was that there was no need for him to get up. No cows to milk. No pigs to feed. No job. No need to work, though he had spent more last evening than he should, but it had been worth it later.

As the sky began to lighten he had had enough of lying about in bed. He pulled on his clothes and dashed water over his face in the sink at the end of the passage. Down in the bar all was still quiet as he let himself out into the fresh air away from the stink of tobacco and beer.

The first thing was to find the docks and ask about ship sailings. He had got a rough idea last evening which direction to go in, and soon got a glimpse over the roof tops of the funnels and masts of the great ships down at the docks.

The only thing was to ask and get advice where to go to get passage. As he came onto the waterfront he was amazed at the activity happening in front of him. The dock edge was lined with vast steel ships, most seemed to be loading or unloading cargo of some sort: crates, bundles, sacks, packages of every size and description. On the dock wagons, barrows and trolleys were moving in and out of the warehouse doors, pushed, pulled and sweated over by a mass of men. Hal stood and watched for several minutes. The shore-side cranes and ships' derricks moved in a continual ballet of dipping into the vast dungeons of the ships' holds. It reminded him of an ants' nest.

"Excuse me, Sir," Hal stopped one of the 'ants' as he came past, "I am wanting to go to America. Where do I go to buy a ticket?"

"Ha, ha," the 'ant' laughed deeply. "You'm one of them country boys wanting to go off an' make your fortune I'll be bound. Where did you want to go?"

"As I said, America. I don't know where else there is that I could go."

| SIX

"Look, son. There is ships going from here to all sorts of places, all over the world. If you wants my advice I should go and talk to them at White Funnel. Go along here for another couple hundred yards and you can't miss 'em."

"Thanks, Sir. I will do that."

Sure enough, the White Funnel building could not be missed: Three stories of imposing stone-built splendour. It looked pretty daunting until Hal saw a doorway marked "General Enquiries." If he didn't ask he would get nowhere. He pushed through the doorway and was startled by the bell, which clanged overhead as the door opened. Opposite was a counter with an elderly clerk behind it, gazing down at a ledger in front of him, pen poised in his hand.

"Yes?" he asked of Hal without looking up.

"I want to go to America" Hal replied, without much confidence after his conversation with the 'ant' earlier.

"Oh, do you now, young man," the clerk replied, at last glancing up and looking at Hal over the top of his pince-nez. "And where do you wish to go?"

" Where do your ships go in America?"

"Boston, New York, and further south. I expect you want New York, though, by the looks of you," he said more kindly, "emigrating are you? Make your fortune no doubt, or so you hope."

"That's the idea, Sir! When will the next ship be leaving that I could travel on, and what will it cost me?" Hal said enthusiastically.

"Now don't get ahead of yourself, young man, I did not say that we had a ship. They don't run like trains you know."

"Oh, I see, I thought you had ships going to the Americas all the time."

"Yes we do, but not all of them carry the likes of you. Mostly they are just taking cargo and every now and again we have one carrying passengers, and usually they take emigrants in steerage as well. However, we will not have one leaving for another six weeks."

"Oh, I can't wait that long, I would have run out of money long before that. I could work my passage, if that would help."

"Oh no, that's not possible. You have no experience of the sea, and anyway you don't have a seaman's card."

"I don't mind work" Hal replied feeling all his confidence draining away.

"I can't help you. I would suggest that you go up to Liverpool, there are plenty of immigrant ships sailing from there. Wait a minute, let me look up in the Ports Directory of Sailings for you." He pushed his pince-nez up his nose and began to thumb slowly through a dog-eared broadsheet, stopping to lick his thumb between pages. "Yes, here you are: S.S. *England* sailing next week for New York via Queenstown. Well, there you are. Get yourself up to Liverpool and good luck to you young sir."

"Thank you very much, you have been most helpful. How do I get to Liverpool though?"

"You really are the country boy! Take a train to London and then get another on the London and North Western Railway. You ask at the station though, they will direct you."

The clerk looked down back to the ledger he had been studying.

Hal was feeling rather foolish by now. Of course he had heard of Liverpool and knew it was up north somewhere. He picked up his bag and decided the sooner he was away from here and had got his ship organised the better.

The journey to London was as enthralling as the previous one had been from Exeter. The great station at Waterloo amazed him, in fact the whole of London amazed him, but at the same time it made him feel very small and ignorant. He had never seen so many people in all his life, in spite of the fact it was by now quite late in the day; if Southampton had been busy then he did not know what to make of this place.

By dint of continually asking people, firstly from where he should catch a train for Liverpool, and then getting directions as he walked across the great city, he eventually arrived at Euston Station. By now he felt mentally and physically exhausted. Not from his exertions (he was well used to long days of farm work), but from the excitement and crowds of people he had had round him all day; not to mention his indulgence of the night before in not just the beer. He pulled his coat around him and settled down to spend the night on a station bench; not the most comfortable of beds, but he was young and dropped straight off like a puppy.

An early train the next morning and he was at Liverpool's Lime Street Station by late afternoon. Once again he asked the way towards the docks, but did find the locals quite difficult to understand. They had a very pronounced local accent and way of speech, but then in the course of conversation over a glass of beer and a piece of pie, he gathered that his Devon burr caused some amusement as well. Once again he found cheap lodgings, he did not need another night of roughing it. This time he resolved not to get involved in a drinking bout or a liaison with the opposite sex.

The next morning he found the S.S.*England* without too much trouble.

"I wish to take passage in the ship when it sails, please," he asked the sailor standing at the end of the gangplank.

"Where's your pass then and you can't board for a couple of days."

"I don't have one yet. I thought I would be able to get a ticket as I went in, like on a coach."

" Well you can't just walk on board like that, you know. You must have a ticket and the only way to get that is to try at the office in the street behind these buildings." He sighed deeply as if he had been through all this a hundred times, and how could people be so stupid. He continued more kindly, "You just go get your pass, that's from the National Steamship Company, they will tell you about boarding and such like."

The office turned out to be a twin of the Southampton shipping office, even down to the clerk behind the desk.

"I would like a ticket for passage in the S.S.*England*, please."

The clerk sucked his teeth with an inhalation of breath and looked doubtful. Hal's heart sank to his boots.

"Well would you now, and what if we are full up for this voyage?"

"Surely you must have room for one more in a big ship like that."

The clerk sucked his teeth again and flipped over the pages of the ledger in front of him.

"Steerage, I presume by the looks of you," he said rather unkindly. "Now let me see. We do have a place on '3' deck, if you want it, that's at the bottom of the accommodation. Though Lord knows why I call it accommodation."

"Yes, yes please, that will do fine for me." Hal was only too pleased to take anything. "How much will that be?"

"That will be the princely sum of five guineas all found, two meals a day."

Hal scrabbled about in his pockets and came up with five one guinea coins. He wondered ruefully how much he had left. He knew he had several five pound notes bundled up in a bag hanging on a string round his neck and safely inside his undershirt.

"There, that's your pass for boarding and that's your receipt for the payment. Don't lose them. You can board from noon tomorrow but make sure you are on board by midnight. After that time you will have missed your berth and no money back, and don't arrive at the gangplank drunk."

He looked back down to his papers and lists and the conversation and information was obviously over as he ignored Hal standing there.

"Thank you." Hal muttered softly so as not to disturb the clerk's 'important work'. He touched his cap as he turned to go, not that it appeared to have been noticed.

7

On the dot of noon the next day Hal was at the foot of the gangway of the S.S.*England*, presented his pass and was allowed on board. He was directed down two steep narrow stairways along what seemed like a maze of passageways and into a room dimly lit by two bare weak electric lights bulbs. Running through the centre was a long scrubbed wooden table with benches on each side. Down the walls of the room were three tiers of wooden bunks, each with a rough straw mattress. The top bunks barely gave room for the occupant to slide in let alone be able to sit up.

At the moment Hal was the only occupant of this 'black hole' so he had the choice of which bunk to claim. He decided that having been told how full the ship would be, it would be better to be near the doorway, but on the other hand this would be the busiest and noisiest. Eventually he chose a bottom bunk about a third of the way down one side, threw his bag onto it and sat down on the bench opposite to consider his surroundings. A rough count of the bunks revealed that when full this room would house about 120 people, it was going to be quite a squash.

Soon Hal was joined by others, mostly of his own age but with some older men as well. They mainly arrived singly but there was the occasional family group. Hal, with his outgoing manner, was soon in conversation with several of them. The mixture of dialects and accents was intriguing. Hal spoke to men from all parts of the north of England, a few from the south like him (nobody from Devon though), but the bulk of them seemed to come from north of the border such as Glasgow and the Highlands.

By late afternoon the flow of new arrivals had ceased. The room (which Hal had been told was a cabin) was less than half full. His new acquaintants agreed that with that number it was not going to be too bad; this comment was made to a passing member of the crew, who laughed.

"Enjoy it while you still can then. You wait till we reach Queenstown, then the whole place will fill up with Paddies."

Hal decided that it was time to go exploring the ship. He soon realised that there was another similar cabin just across the passage and that the two of them shared a rather foetid washroom with six sinks and the same number of doorless cubicles. This would be a crowd.

On further investigation he discovered another pair of cabins similar to his, and a stairway down, marked 'Women only', all on the same deck. So if the women's cabin was similar to the men's that meant that there could be over 700 people squashed in on that one deck down in the bowels of the ship.

He moved on up to the next deck which appeared to be similar but with much more room in the cabins and he guessed probably housing another 300 souls.

The main deck above was open round the sides with deck housing down the middle, a saloon, smart cabins and the officers quarters, all very obviously off limits to the likes of him.

Rising above were three masts and one thin funnel behind the small raised bridge.

Hal leaned on the rail watching a smartly dressed family coming up the gangway followed by three crew carrying their mass of suitcases, hatboxes and other luggage. The family and their luggage all disappeared into the deck housing.

"Alright for some, ain't it." Hal had not noticed the middle-aged man who had come to lean on the rail next to him.

"Yes, if you have the money," he commented wryly. "Are you one of the crew or, like me, are you a passenger? Hal Slater's the name."

"Arnie Baker. Pleased to make your acquaintance. For my sins I am a stoker on this old tub."

"Oh. You must know all about the ship then? I am going to America to find a job working on machinery. Tell me about this ship's engines."

"I don't know that I can tell you much. I just shovel coal into the boiler! Actually the engine is a Compound driving a single screw, obviously steam-driven. We make about 10 knots. Do you understand what I mean by a knot?"

"No I don't, but I have heard the word," Hal admitted, feeling rather foolish.

"I am not surprised if you have had nothing to do with the sea and ships. It's the way we measure speed at sea or the time to go for a nautical mile which is slightly less than an ordinary mile. This ship was built in 1865. She is 3308 tons, 375 feet long. I only know all this 'cos there's a brass plate fixed on the front of the bridge," Arnie recounted with a smile. "Well, I must get along now. Got to keep the home fires burning, as they say."

They sailed for Queenstown soon after midnight. Hal had decided to stay up to watch their departure and trip down the Mersey to the open sea. There would be plenty of time later when there would be nothing to see other than the ocean.

Two tugs pushed and pulled at bow and stern to get the ship away from the dockside. Puffing steam and clouds of black smoke which eddied up to join the clouds coming from the ship's single funnel and being wafted away on the strong breeze into the dark night sky.

Hal resolved to seek out his new acquaintance, Arnie Baker, at the first opportunity, to see if he could arrange for him to go below to see the engine and boiler rooms at some time.

The next morning Hal was not sure that he wanted to do anything but die. Along with most of the others in his cabin he did not feel at all well, suffering from severe seasickness. The cabin just would not keep still; the ship seemed to be twisting and turning the whole time. One minute standing on its head, the next lying over sideways, and in between corkscrewing.

At last the smell and unpleasantness down below drove him to the upper deck into the fresh air. Surprisingly to him, he felt much improved as the wind cleared his head. He very quickly realised that it was not a good idea to stand on the windward side of the deck where the strong wind drove the spray over the bows and swept it down the deck as the ship butted into the rough sea. He moved to the other side, pulling his topcoat tightly round him, and squatted down in the lee of the deckhouse. He was fascinated by the waves and the way the ship pushed the sea aside to create waves of its own, which swished and tossed as they met and fought with others. A stream of black smoke was dragged from the top of the funnel by the wind, which howled and screeched through the rigging.

Two days later they crept into the dock at Queenstown, in southern Ireland, as the last of the light faded away behind the lowering rain clouds. It looked a dismal place to Hal, but as they were not allowed ashore it did not really matter. However, he did have a stab of conscience that he had not written to Sarah to tell her that he was on his way to his new life. He begged paper and an envelope and scribbled her a short note, which he was assured would be landed and put into the mail. How long it would take to reach her he had no idea, but he had tried and would write again when they arrived.

The following morning, as the cabin occupants were eating what passed for breakfast - tea and a hunk of bread - which they had had to fetch from the steerage passengers' galley in an oversized kettle and tray, there was an influx of new passengers.

The cabin was soon full of the noise of gentle Irish brogue as the new arrivals sorted themselves out into the empty bunks. They were almost all young men in their twenties. Hal's first impression was that they came from all sorts of trades; some were pale in appearance as if they were city lads with hands that were not used to manual work but to some indoor occupation, while others had weather-beaten complexions and gnarled, scarred hands from outside work. However, they were all cooped up together and there would be time to discover their histories during the long voyage.

The top bunk of Hal's trio had been empty for the trip from Liverpool. One of the new arrivals threw his bag onto it and turned to Hal. He was a lad of about Hal's age, possibly a couple of years younger, well built with dark hair cut really short, standing a bit under six foot.

"The top of the morning to you. I am Jason O'Kelly from Waterford. It looks as if we will be travelling together." He stuck out his hand to Hal. He did not really fit either of the categories that Hal had put the new arrivals into. It was definitely a hand used to hard work but Jason's voice was of a more educated man.

"Hello, I am Hal Slater. I've got the bottom bunk. We got a good choice at boarding, as there were not that many of us. I started my journey in Devon."

They chatted for a while about this and that, until Jason pulled a pocket watch from his waistcoat.

"How time flies when one meets new friends! I must be away up on deck to make sure my sister has settled in alright."

He left hurriedly but turned as he went through the doorway.

"Why don't you come up and meet her?"

"Yes, I will do that. Welcome her aboard this old tub! Anyway I could do with some fresh air. It does get pretty foetid down here, especially when the hatches are shut."

They climbed up to the upper deck. Jason had a quick look round and saw no sign of his sister, so they leant on the rail by the doorway watching crates of cargo being hoisted aboard by the forward derrick of the ship and lowered skilfully into the hold.

They both turned as a young woman came up behind them.

"There you are! I came up ten minutes ago and there was no sign of you," she scolded gently.

"I am sorry. I got talking. Let me introduce you to Hal. We nearly share a bunk! Hal, this is my sister Maggie."

While he spoke Hal had been 'looking over' the young woman in front of him. She was shorter than Jason by a couple of inches but had the same dark hair hanging to her shoulders, pulled loosely back with a green ribbon to behind her ears. The ribbon matched the colour of her eyes, he noticed. Her narrow waist accentuated her well formed but not over-large bosom snugged in by her dress, secured tightly at her neck by a large brooch.

"Pleased to meet you, I am sure." Her gaze did not waver, as she looked him directly in the eye. Her face broke into an infectious grin. "I take it that by saying you nearly share a bunk they must be like those in my cabin: Squashed in and piled three high."

"Yes, you are right. It is a squash and it will be even worse now you Irish have arrived. I find I have spent most of the day up here on deck where it is more pleasant."

"Heh! We Irish don't take up that much room, you know!"

"Oh, I am sorry, I did not mean to be rude." Hal blushed deeply in his confusion.

"Don't you worry your sweet self over it now, I was only joking. I had forgotten that the English do not have a sense of humour."

Hal began to get his hackles up before he realised he was having his leg pulled again. He broke into laughter and Jason and Maggie joined in.

Hal decided that he was going to enjoy the journey to America with this young couple, especially with Maggie.

As soon as the cargo loading was completed they left Queenstown and turned west towards America. The new arrivals and some of the originals succumbed to seasickness again, but Hal, Jason and Maggie were spared. Their friendship blossomed as they spent each day sitting out of the wind discussing their plans for the future and recounting their lives to date.

Maggie was two years older than Jason at twenty-three. They had lived all their lives in Waterford, a small town on the Southeast corner of Ireland. Their father had established a builders business in the town, which Jason had been expected to join on leaving school aged fourteen. His heart had not been in it as he had a yearning to make more of himself and felt he would like a career in law. Consequently the last few years had not been happy ones. Now, rather like Hal, he had decided to make a new life for himself and, if possible, study to be a lawyer in a new country.

Maggie, who had for years been more like a mother to Jason, their mother having died when she was six, decided she would give up her job working in a haberdashery shop to travel with him. Hal could see that they were a very close brother and sister.

Their ambitions were vague. They would see what turned up once they landed in New York, very much like Hal's 'plans'.

8

The trio's days followed the same pattern. They would meet up on deck to stroll round for exercise, weather permitting. They all found the tedium of doing nothing tiring. They were after all young people used to doing active jobs.

Four days out from Queenstown six men in the next cabin to Hal's and Jason's went down with vomiting and diarrhoea. It did not seem to be another bout of seasickness. Maggie reported that women in the female cabins were suffering the same symptoms as well. The next day a lot more men were struck down, and later that evening Jason added his name to the growing list.

The sickness had been reported to the crew and word had reached the first mate, who was apparently responsible for the health of crew and passengers. He came down to the cabins to tell them that he suspected they had an epidemic of cholera. He assured them that it was not catching, provided they were careful with their hygiene. Hal thought to himself that considering the state of the toilets and washroom that it might be difficult. The galley would boil all drinking water, and they would take extra care with the food. The important thing was to keep drinking. The greatest danger was from becoming dehydrated, Hal discovered from the mate.

Conditions down below had been bad enough before the outbreak, now they became appalling.

"Jason, I will swap bunks with you" Hal suggested the first evening of Jason's sickness.

"No, Hal, you were here first at Liverpool and you chose a bottom bunk, so you keep it."

"Look Jason, don't be so stupid. You are having to climb down from the top every time you need the 'heads', which seems to be pretty often. Apart from which I don't want you caught short and unable to control yourself when you are half way down! I insist." Hal tried to make something humorous out of what was in fact a serious situation.

"Alright. I suppose it makes sense. Hal, will you try and see Maggie? I am worried about her all on her own. I just pray that she has not been struck down as well."

Hal did not see Maggie when he went on deck. He was rather concerned about this, but perhaps she was trying to help the women in her cabin that were sick, as Hal was doing in his cabin. Though Lord knows there was little that he could do other than bring them water. He did manage to get a young girl from the other women's cabin to bring him word of Maggie; she was all right apparently. Jason was obviously relieved at this news when Hal reported back to him.

The next morning Jason was very much worse. Like the others he was vomiting and losing liquid at an alarming rate; this in its turn caused very painful muscle cramps. He was already looking only half the man he had been 24 hours earlier; his eyes were sunken and black rimmed, the flesh seemed to have shrunk from his face which was lined like an old man's. In between the cramps he was shivering with cold one minute and the next breaking out in a hot sweat.

Hal had persuaded the cook in the galley to give him a small quantity of sugar, baking powder and salt which he dissolved in water and made Jason drink as much as he could without continually bringing it up again. Hal had had a sudden flash of memory that it was his mother's remedy for violent sickness whenever he or her other children had been taken ill, and it was the treatment they had given to calves if they had diarrhoea from taking too much milk.

Mid-morning one of Hal's cabin mates brought word down from above that Maggie was on deck and worried about her brother. Jason had fallen into a disturbed sleep and Hal felt he could leave him for a few minutes.

As soon as he came on deck Maggie ran up to him, gripped him by the elbows with a worried expression on her face.

"Hal, thank the Lord you are alright, but what of my brother, Jason? How is he? Please tell me that he does not have the sickness."

"No Maggie, I can't do that. He is not good at all, I fear. You have seen the symptoms, I am sure. He has the cramps and sickness and is getting weaker by the hour. I am doing what I can for him but fear he is losing strength. At the moment he is sleeping. I wish I could give you better news."

"Oh Hal, thank you for your help. Do you think there is any way I can see him?"

"They are very strict about women going to the men's cabins, as you know. I will speak to one of the officers when I can and see if they will allow it in the circumstances. How are things in your cabin?"

"Awful. Half of them are sick and there does not seem to be any help from anybody. Will we all get it do you think?"

| EIGHT

"No, I am told that it does not affect everybody; but of those that do get it, some will be much worse than others and it will take some. It is not catching like a cold or such like and is not spread by vermin on the body like the plague, but is caught from it getting into one's guts. Be especially careful of washing in clean water. The food from the galley - we just have to hope that they are cooking it really well."

"It won't take Jason, will it? I would rather die than him."

"Maggie, I don't know, but I must tell you he does not look well. I am doing everything I can for him. We can only trust in the Lord. If you believe in a God, then now is the time to pray to him for his help. Now let's go and see if we can find an officer to give you permission to visit Jason."

They climbed up the ladder to the upper deck where the cabins were for the rich, an area that as steerage class they were not allowed to enter. They did get some disapproving looks, but after asking several crew-members and being told to go to higher authority each time, they eventually tracked down the first mate. He was sympathetic to the request and gave his permission for Maggie to have ten minutes with her brother, so long as it was this morning. He did not want young ladies in the men's cabins any later than midday. Hal did not comment but thought to himself that in the circumstances a high moral code was not something to worry about.

"Come on young lady, let's go now before he changes his mind." Hal led her down below decks without them exchanging another word. Jason was hot with fever when they arrived at his bunk side. Hal's heart twisted when he saw the pained expression on Maggie's face as she got her first look at her brother. She knelt down on the dirty deck to try and comfort him. Hal left them together while he went to fetch water to bathe Jason's sweating face. When he returned he passed the bowl to Maggie to cool him as best as she could. They were oblivious to time and were surprised that two hours had passed when the Bo'sun came in and in a gruff voice asked what Maggie was doing in the men's quarters. Hal quickly explained that they had permission for her to visit her sick brother. He insisted that she should return to her own quarters. She left reluctantly, arranging that Hal would meet her to give her regular reports on Jason's condition.

When she had gone, Jason half raised himself, beckoned Hal to bend close to him and took his hand in a vice-like grip as he whispered "Hal, I have not known you for long but I do believe you to be a good man. I am asking you to look after Maggie for me, as I don't think I am going to make it. I don't know what she would do on her own in a strange country and we have no money for a return voyage to take her back home. I know it is a lot to ask of a man, but I have no one else to turn to. You will do as I ask, please."

"Don't be so silly, man. In a few days you will be up again, perhaps a bit weak, but some good fresh sea air will soon put you to rights." Hal said this, he hoped with conviction, but he felt that Jason was going to have a job to pull through.

"Hal, I pray that you are right, but please promise me that if the worst does happen you will do as I ask."

"Yes Jason, of course I will. I will see her alright and see that she gets safely to wherever she wants ."

Jason sank back onto the mattress with a look of relief on his face.

The first death came that evening, closely followed by three more overnight. The cholera continued to take its toll the next day with five more including two women, one only a twelve-year-old. The ship was stopped before dark to allow the Captain to conduct a short funeral service before the bodies were slid silently into the sea. An air of complete desolation hung over the ship and a fear of the unknown as to when this pestilence would end.

Hal met by arrangement twice that day with Maggie on deck. He discouraged her from paying another visit to Jason; he was now only a shadow of the young man who had come aboard ship at Queenstown. In the evening Jason seemed to slip into a coma and apart from unintelligible mumblings did not speak again or respond to Hal in any way. Soon after midnight he gave up the struggle and passed away. Hal covered him and went to find the first officer to report the death and seek permission for Maggie to visit once again to say her goodbyes to her brother. He got word down to Maggie and she came straight on deck to him.

"Maggie, I am afraid Jason is gone. He left us about ten minutes ago, very peacefully at the end."

Hal found this such a difficult thing to say. He had had to cope with his father's death, which had been bad enough, but never had he had to break the news to someone else. While waiting for Maggie he had been trying to find the words that would break the news in the most comforting way.

"Oh Hal. Poor Jason. Why did it have to be him that was taken? He was such a good and kind man. I really brought him up you know, ever since mother died when he was six and I was eight…"

She continued talking non-stop with hardly a moment to draw breath.

"Maggie," Hal interrupted her flood of words, " let the tears come. Don't try and hold them back, it's only natural and nothing to be ashamed of. Come here, let me comfort you." He took her shoulders and her green eyes bored into his before she came willingly into his arms burying her face in his shoulder. After a moment Hal felt her wracked with grief as she shuddered and the tears came flooding out of her. They sat on the deck for the rest of the night, huddled

EIGHT

together in the lea of the funnel, speaking only intermittently, each with their own thoughts, wrapped in Hal's topcoat.

The next morning the ship was stopped once again and the bodies were slipped quietly from under the Union flag which covered them, while the Captain conducted a short service of burial. Maggie was by now dry-eyed, but with great dark rings under them from her sleepless night and grief. Hal stood at her side with just a hand on her elbow, hoping he was giving her some support at what must be a very low moment for her. He had only known Jason for a few days but was very conscious of the reassurance he had given him before he died. It did put Hal in an awkward spot to have the responsibility of Maggie to look after. Of course she might well want to make her own way once they reached America and might want nothing to do with him. He decided that in the very near future he must bring the subject up and clear the air so to speak.

This proved to be the last time the ship had to stop for a burial. Many passengers remained ill, but there were no more deaths and the word was that they were all beginning to make a recovery. The word got round that they were now headed for Lawler's Island, Halifax, in Newfoundland to go to the quarantine anchorage before they would be allowed on to New York. Only once they had been cleared of the disease would they be allowed to continue their journey.

Hal realised that there was plenty of time to make a decision rather than dash into bringing up the subject of their future and Maggie made no mention of her plans. He was uncertain what he was going to do himself, let alone have to organise life for another. Though he had to admit that he and Maggie seemed to get along well together. They spent the days on deck talking some of the time, at others just content with the other's company or their own thoughts.

Once at Halifax Hal decided he had to bring the subject up so as to clear his mind of his obligation to Jason.

"Maggie, I want to talk about Jason for a moment, if that is not too painful for you?"

"No, of course not. We have been mentioning him the last few days as we chatted. It has been of great help to me to get over my loss. I will always remember him with great love, but he is gone now and I must move on with my life. I know it is what he would have wanted me to do. What was it you wished to say about him?" She seemed very positive, he thought.

Hal took a deep breath. He had not come to any sensible conclusions and was not sure how to approach the subject. He still did not know what he wanted, but he had made a promise to Jason, even if it had only been the right thing to say to the dying man at the time. Hal had always been brought up to keep his promises and this was not the moment to change, his conscience would not allow it.

"The day before he died, while he was able to still think clearly, after you had been down to see him that first time, you remember? He felt that he was not going to recover and made me promise him something, which of course I did. Although we had not known each other for long I did not really have any option than to ease his mind of his worry."

"Come on Hal. What was this promise? though I think I can guess, knowing Jason as I did," she said in her definite no-nonsense way.

"Oh goodness. I have not put this very well. Maggie, please let me finish. I am finding this hard enough as it is without you trying to out-guess me."

"Very well then. I am sorry, I should not have interrupted you," she said, tossing her head in the air and making out that she was offended at being reprimanded. Hal carried on regardless, ignoring her little act of pique.

"He made me promise that I would look after you and see you alright," he hurried on before Maggie could interrupt again. "Of course I will do that as best as I can if that is what you wish, but you may have made other plans, in which case we will go our own ways." Hal blushed deeply in his confusion at trying to express himself.

"Oh Hal, you are a sweet boy to be sure. I hope it has not been a worry to you the last few days. If you really want to know, Jason told me he was going to ask you this when you took me down to see him. Of course you must not feel you have to look out for me. I am a big girl and will be quite able to look after myself, though Lord knows what I will do; but there must be suitable jobs in a big place like America. Of course, if the worst comes to the worst I can always go on the street and sell myself!"

Hal turned to her with a look of horror and then saw the laughter twinkling out of her green eyes at him. This was more like the Maggie he had come to know before Jason had been struck down.

"Maggie O'Kelly, you are a tease and a minx. You should not talk in such a way. It's not right that a lady like you should speak of such things. Now let's be serious for just a minute for this is important. I suggest that once we get ashore in New York we stick together and see what turns up. We will both need support at that time in our new venture, unless of course you plan to return home?"

"That's a laugh. I certainly have not enough money for the journey back, even if I was prepared to be humiliated in returning home so soon. Anyway, I could not possibly face that journey again. No, your idea of sticking together seems a good one. If at any time we decide to go our own ways then there will be nothing lost."

| EIGHT

Hal decided that he could not ask for a better companion, in fact over the last couple of weeks he had grown quite fond of this handsome, outspoken girl. He would always know exactly where he stood with her, other than when she was making fun of him, which was quite often. More often than not she caught him out.

One day dragged into another as they were held at Halifax in the quarantine station. Everybody became more and more bored with no way of knowing how long they would be held there. A close check was kept on the ship to make sure nobody tried to escape ashore, though it would have been a risky thing to try as they were anchored well off shore and the sea temperature was probably near to freezing. The officers and crew were not giving anything away, even if they had more information. Fights became more common amongst both the men and women, usually over accusations of petty stealing or arguments getting out of hand. Those that had been ill made a slow recovery, though the diet and conditions were not exactly a help for convalescence. A near-mutiny was only just averted when the captain changed his mind after ordering that each passenger would have to pay an extra two guineas because of the extended voyage. The steerage passengers were travelling to their new life with virtually nothing as it was; another expense of two guineas would have been a very large proportion of what they possessed.

Eventually, after two weeks, the Port Health Officials gave them a clean bill of health. The anchor was dragged clanking up from the muddy sea bed and once again a plume of black smoke issued from the funnel. The air of depression that had hung over the ship since the onset of the cholera seemed immediately to be lifted. Laughter was once again heard and there was a continual chatter of excitement. Past differences were soon forgotten. Groups of people got together discussing what they planned to do once they had landed.

Hal and Maggie were no different to the others.

"Hal, me boyo! Tell me what's a big strong lad like you going to do in New York? There won't be too many cows to milk in a big city."

"You are right there, me bonny lass! Anyways I am not just any old farm boy I would have you know. I am a skilled mechanic of farm machinery, and I expect some respect from a young girl like you straight out of an Irish bog."

"You cheeky little pip-squeak. I have half a mind to put you over my knee and give you a good walloping." She came up close to him wagging her finger in his face. The trouble was, the top of her head only came up to his chin so she had to look right up to see his eyes. On an impulse she grabbed him by both ears; as he started away, she pulled his head down and kissed him hard on the mouth. They drew apart quickly, Hal with a look of surprise on his face, Maggie beginning to blush profusely.

"Hal, I am sorry. I don't know what came over me. You must think me a real hussy," she stammered, her dark hair tumbling over her eyes.

In the short time Hal had known her he had never seen her so apologetic and lacking in confidence. He was soon over the surprise, but found himself surprising himself as he stepped up to her and took her by the shoulders.

"Yes, Maggie O'Kelly, you are a little hussy, I was right before. I am going to punish you for what you have done," he said in his sternest voice with a glare.

He leant down and gave as good as he had got with another hard lingering kiss. Maggie did not try to pull away once she had recovered from the shock of his riposte, in fact her arms reached up round his neck. After a moment they reluctantly pulled apart, but Hal did not let go of her shoulders.

"I have been wanting to do that for several days now," he said breathlessly.

"Oh Hal! I must admit that I have felt the same. I have felt safe and secure with you since Jason left us, but I think I felt in shock at what happened and you were there to support me. We have only known each other for a few weeks and that has been in the cramped surroundings of this hell ship. I don't think this is quite the time or place to make any great commitments to each other. Please don't be offended. I must have time. I should never have kissed you like that."

Hal's heart sank. A moment ago he was on the top of the world, now he had come crashing down. Not that he had ever considered Maggie as anyone but a friend until that impulsive kiss, but at that moment it was as if he had had a vision, now no more. He had to tough it out though.

"For heaven's sake, Maggie my girl, you don't imagine that one kiss should lead to anything more permanent, I hope. I have kissed a lot of girls in my time and you have, I am sure, been kissed by a lot of boys."

Hal realised he was beginning to bluster a bit and was about to make a fool of himself; however, he was feeling that he would like things to develop from that kiss.

Anyway, he was abruptly cut short.

"What sort of a girl do you think I am, Hal Slater, and I am not 'your' girl. I have certainly not been kissed by lots of boys. I am not free and easy as the likes of some I could name," she said indignantly as the colour rose in her cheeks. She hoicked up her skirts, turned smartly on her heel and flounced off.

Oh goodness, now I have gone and spoilt our whole relationship, thought Hal. He leant on the rail, staring sadly out over the tossing waves. What am I to say to her when we meet next? She is the only friend I have on this side of the ocean. Suddenly he felt very lonely.

He turned at a light touch on his shoulder. Maggie stood there, the blush gone from her cheeks, in fact looking rather pale. Her hair blowing out free in

| *EIGHT*

the wind, her green eyes looking directly into his. Looking more lovely than he had seen her in the short time they had known each other.

"Hal, I am sorry, I should not have flounced off like that. It was very silly. I was behaving like the quick-tempered girl that I am. Like a spoilt..." Hal interrupted.

"No, Maggie dear. I should not have said what I did. It was unkind. I think we were both a little carried away with what happened before and rather surprised. Let's just slow down a bit and go on with what has been a very good friendship."

9

Mid-morning a few days later all passengers were on deck as they steamed up the Ambrose Channel and slowly into the Lower Bay of the Hudson River.

Hal and Maggie stood squeezed onto the rail as everybody caught their first glimpse of the country that was to be their new homeland. First impression was rather disappointing; of a mist or smoke covered low-lying grey land mass spreading out in all directions in front of them. As they drew nearer, the land enclosed them more tightly as they entered The Narrows, and then widened out again as they got into Upper New York Bay.

Now excitement began to rise as the view up the East River opened out and they were able to see the almost completed Brooklyn Suspension Bridge. The word seemed to spread that they were looking at Manhattan Island in front of them to the left of the East River, Brooklyn to their right and Staten Island to the left. The ship steamed slowly up the Hudson River and they were able to get a better view of the great growing city of New York. It now looked more exciting as they were able to pick out buildings in more detail. They were headed for the docks, which lined the banks of the river as far as the eye could see up the west side of Manhattan.

Two tugs came puffing and smoking out to guide them in to the dockside, bows to the land. Ropes were thrown and cables hauled across by the long-shore men, with much banter from the crew. Laughter turned to a great cheer from the passengers, as one of the men fell onto his back into a puddle as he dragged on a rope. The mood was one of elation now that the horrendous journey was over at last.

There was a sudden exodus from deck as everybody rushed below to get together their meagre belongings, expecting to be allowed ashore as soon as the gangplanks were in place. Hal and Maggie were no exception as they stood together amongst the crowd. It turned out that it was to be a long process, however. They were not to be allowed to flood off the ship and just disappear

| NINE

into the vastness of this great continent. A long queue wound its way down the gangplank and into a warehouse. Trestle tables were set up down each side. Behind these were clerks and immigration officers who had it all under control; they had done it a thousand times before. The queue was divided in two, women to the right, men to the left.

Hal reached the head of the queue at long last. He could see that Maggie was already a third of the way down the tables on her side. He wondered if they would ever be able to meet up together again.

"Name and initial?" Hal's mind was drawn back to the clerk in front of him. He did not quite understand the abrupt question put to him in such an unusual accent.

"I haven't got all day, boy. Name and initial."

"Harold Slater. My surname is Slater," he added quickly as he noticed the clerk start to write down Harold as his surname.

The clerk looked up with contempt as he passed across the form he had written these details on.

"Next. Move on you."

"Nationality?" The next clerk added this to the form. Gradually the line shuffled up the row of tables adding information as they went. Hal did not have a chance to glance over to the other side of the room, so he had no idea what had happened to Maggie.

"Where are you going to lodge?" This said in a more kindly voice by a man who looked as if he could be a priest.

"I have no idea at the moment" Hal stammered. He was feeling really rather insignificant after all the interrogation along the line of tables.

"Here, take this. You may be able to find a place to sleep and get a meal at this address." He passed over a small card.

"Good luck."

The final table seemed to be enclosed by screens. Hal pushed his way when told.

"Stick your tongue out… Lift your arms up… Now drop your pants."

Hal looked in surprise at the man in a white coat, a doctor he presumed, and thought he must have misunderstood him again.

"Trousers, then, I suppose you call them."

Hal continued to look at him with horror. Nobody had ever asked him to do that before. His mother was the only one who had ever seen those parts when she scrubbed his back on bath night. Of course there was the barmaid in Southampton, but then it had been dark and they were in bed.

"Come on, I have seen it all before, you know. I don't imagine you are much different from anyone else."

Hal slipped his braces off and reluctantly lowered his trousers, only to have his crown jewels held firmly.

"Cough." Hal did as he was told but really feeling he would rather take a swing at the doctor.

"OK. Pull them up again." The doctor added his signature to the form, and passed it to Hal.

"On your way then. You are free to go."

Hal pushed through the curtain again as he slipped back into his jacket and topcoat. He was directed out of the warehouse into the small lean-to at the back where he was relieved to find Maggie waiting.

"Am I glad to see you. That really was quite an experience, I have never been treated like that before," Hal greeted her.

"Why? What did they do to you? I was most embarrassed, but they told me I could not enter the country without all the checks. I blush at even thinking about it," Maggie said looking away.

"I am certainly not going to tell you what happened."

"Nor me you."

They both burst into laughter as they kept their own secrets.

One final stamp on their forms and they had been cleared to enter the city as new citizens of the United States of America.

NEW YORK AND WEST
November 1882

10

They picked up their bags and walked out onto the street behind the warehouse into the bustle of Manhattan.

"What now? We have no plans. We don't know where to go or what to do. All I have is this card with an address on it." The enormity of their situation struck Hal like a sledgehammer. It had all seemed so easy and exciting up to now.

"I have a card as well, given to me by a kind woman in the registration hall. She said I would be able to get lodgings there. Come on Hal, cheer up. I have a little money left, so we can get something to eat and make plans over the meal. Proper food will be a treat after the rubbish we have had to put up with on the ship."

"Yes, that sounds like a sensible idea. I have money too. I say we should pay for ourselves and then we won't feel indebted to each other. I think we should get away from the docks a bit. There are so many folk just like us round here and they will all be wanting to find work immediately. Ask in which direction we should head for these lodgings."

Hal took Maggie's bag for her and they walked for an hour through the city.

"My feet are beginning to feel really sore. Let's stop at the next bar," Maggie groaned; "I'm not used to these hard roads and so much walking; especially having been shut up on that awful ship for so long."

"Right, let's go in here. It says 'chowder', whatever that is, and ale. I know what that is and I could certainly do with something to wet my whistle." Hal was feeling more cheerful now they had got going.

Chowder turned out to be a sort of fish stew; it was cheap. They were both rather conscious of their lack of much in the way of funds. When it came, with a lump of bread and a pot of ale, they both looked at it hesitantly, glanced up at each other and smiled.

"It looks very similar to what we have got used to the last few weeks... Slop," Hal commented as he tried it. "Actually it's not too bad a taste, so long as one does not look at it."

"Right now what are we going to do? I suggest we find these lodgings for a start, we have to have somewhere for the night." Maggie was being really positive as she pulled out her card and looked at Hal's as he passed it over to her. "The address on them seems to be the same. Presumably boys' and girls' dormitories," she said with a twinkle in her eye. "I would not want to hear you snoring away all night."

Hal became serious as he thought ahead. He was a country lad and was not that taken with big cities. He felt that he needed to get away to the country, where he would be able to practice his skill with farm machinery. Just at the moment he had no idea how to set about it. It had all seemed so easy and idyllic back at Cogwell. What would Maggie want? Although they had decided that they were not dependent on each other.

"What are you going to do, Maggie? Work, I mean."

"I don't really know. I am used to serving in a shop, so I suppose that is the thing for me to start with." After a moment's thought she said "I think we had better see if there is a newspaper or something that would list jobs. Back home that was how people did it."

Hal went up to the bar to ask the customers, leaning with their elbows on the counter, about newspapers.

"Excuse me, Sir, can you recommend a newspaper that advertises jobs?" Hal asked of the grey-haired man sitting in front of him.

"You just off a ship then?" he replied. "I don't know why all of you young people come over here. It just means that work is more difficult for the rest of us to find. Why don't you stay back in your own countries."

Hal was tired, worried and feeling responsible for Maggie. He was usually not short-tempered, but today was different.

"Well, I suppose you have been here for ever then. You don't look as if you are very keen to work, leaning on a bar at this time of day. I only wanted to ask about newspapers." Hal was a big imposing lad. He drew himself up with his fists clenched at his side.

"Well, as a matter of fact I have been here for about fifteen years," the grey-haired man replied as he turned on his stool. He looked Hal up and down, decided that he would be better off staying sitting where he was. Hal turned away, but swung quickly back again as he felt a tap on his shoulder; his fists coming up together ready to protect himself, expecting the worst.

"Hal, come on let's go. It is not worth getting into a fight over such a trivial thing." Maggie pulled at his sleeve to drag him away.

"Wait a minute, young man. You seem to have a bit of spunk about you, and at least you can speak the language, not like some of the Europeans that arrive here.

The grey-haired man beckoned Hal back. He was older looking from his front than had appeared from his back view. A lined pale complexion but with the hint of a smile hovering round his lips. His English speech was good but with a guttural accent, which Hal decided was probably Eastern European of some sort. There were so many nationalities in this big city that it could have been from anywhere in Europe.

"First to put you right on one thing: I do work; I have a good job working at nights. So I have every right to sit at a bar having a quiet drink during the day! Secondly, I may be able to help you."

Hal was somewhat taken aback by this sudden possible solution to their problems.

"I am sorry, Sir. I was too quick to assume you were being critical of us as new arrivals." Hal's flash of temper disappeared as quickly as it had erupted.

"Don't worry about that. I was being critical anyway. I see too many young people like yourselves come off the boats into what they think is the promised land of riches; and then they are disappointed when they discover that life here is a slog and no better than the one they have left. I was one of them myself when I got off the boat, in fact I could not even speak the language. I think from the look and sound of you that you may be different. You sound to me as if you have a lot of determination. Now do you have a trade? And what about you, young lady, I assume you are both together?"

"Oh yes, Sir. We became friends as we travelled on the same ship."

"Which one was that, might I ask?"

"S.S.*England*, Sir."

"Oh yes. Got in this morning. Had a bit of trouble, did you not?"

Hal's impatience was beginning to return with all these questions. He quickly, gruffly, replied before Maggie could speak again.

"Yes. We had 'trouble' as you put it, with cholera. In fact Maggie here lost her brother to it. Now Sir, you said you might be able to help us."

"I am sorry to hear that, Maggie. My condolences. Now you were asking about newspapers. I guess because you think there might be work advertised in them. Well, I am in the printing business and I work for the *Daily Herald*, the biggest paper in the city, though I have to admit probably not the best for finding employment. By the way my name is Baumgarten ... Frederick Baumgarten. Pleased to meet you. This is Maggie I know, and who are you, young man?"

"Hal Slater, Sir, from Devon."

"Yes Sir, I am Maggie, Maggie O'Kelly, from Waterford, Ireland."

"I can tell, easy enough, that you come from the Emerald Isle, my dear," he said easily.

"Now I wonder how that would be?" Maggie replied, flirting outrageously. "And what nationality would you be, Mr Frederick Baumgarten?"

"Why, of course I am American! But when I got on the boat, all those years ago, I had come from Munich, Germany."

Hal was beginning to wonder how long this exchange was going to go on. Did Maggie not realise that they had much more important things to talk about than this nonsense. He interrupted the exchange between them tersely. He was not quite sure whether he trusted this Frederick Baumgarten.

"You asked about my trade? I have worked on my family farm all my life, but my real interest is in machinery and steam engines. I am a good fitter" he said, hoping that this would impress and make him sound less like a country yokel.

"I have worked in haberdashery," Maggie said and quickly added "I also kept the books for my father's building business." This was only partly true. Her father liked her to check the addition after the clerk had totalled it. Her father was a suspicious man and trusted no one. He had no head for figures or writing and could barely read.

"Well, that's interesting. At least you both have some sort of qualification, although, Hal, there is not a great call for farm mechanics in New York!" he said with a twinkle in his eye.

This put Hal off him even further. He was in no mood to be made fun of, but he held his tongue as he could see Maggie giving him sidelong glances.

"Look, I will make some enquiries. Come and see me at the *Herald* offices late tomorrow afternoon, and when I say late, I mean after six!"

"How will we find you there? I expect it is a big place?" Maggie asked.

"Oh, just ask at the front desk for me. Someone will find me or send you in the right direction."

"Thank you for your help, Sir. You have been most kind. We had better get along now and go and find some lodgings. Come on Hal, time to go."

Hal nodded his thanks, turned and followed Maggie outside. As soon as they were out of the swing doors she turned to Hal.

"What was that all about then, Hal Slater?" she asked crossly, turning him round to face her. "It was not like you at all. You were almost rude to Mr Baum-

| TEN

garten, who was only trying to be helpful. I can't think what came over you. I was just having a nice conversation with him and you kept interrupting."

"He rubbed me up the wrong way right from the beginning. I think he was really just interested in you as a pretty young woman. I am not sure we should trust him."

"Now wait a minute. I do believe you were jealous, because he was talking to me." She dissolved into convulsions of laughter, giving him a gentle shove on the chest.

"Don't be so silly. Why should I be jealous of you flirting with him, someone you had only met a few moments before? Anyway, I feel responsible for you after I gave Jason my promise. You know that is the only reason we have stuck together."

This very quickly wiped the laughter from Maggie's face. As soon as he said it Hal regretted the words he had used, it had been thoughtless. He should not have reacted like that. She probably was quite right; he had felt jealous and left out.

"Oh well, if that is the way you feel, I certainly don't want to hold you to something you said to a dying man on the spur of the moment." Her voice trembled slightly but was not raised in anger, rather with a tone of deep hurt and sadness. She took her bag out of his hand, turned, and spoke over her shoulder to him as she started to walk away. "I think it best if we make our own way from now on, Hal. I am going to find somewhere to sleep tonight; I will certainly be going to see Mr Baumgarten tomorrow."

Hal remembered that the saying goes: 'Pride comes before a Fall'. However, he was not going to go running after her in spite of realising that he had been very insensitive. He was not her lackey. If she wanted to get involved with someone, it was not any of his business. He did have pride and it probably was best that they should split up. He did not like the city and he would never find the sort of work he enjoyed here.

On the other hand he was enjoying Maggie's company and it was nice to have someone to share worries with... He did feel responsible about his promise to Jason as well... If he was really honest with himself he knew there was a lot more than just a good friendship on his side, and he suspected she felt the same... Oh well, let her come looking for him. She knew where he would be staying tonight at the hostel... Hell! She still had the address of the lodgings; and for the life of him he could not remember it. Why had she not given his card back to him? She probably had kept it on purpose to spite him.

All these thoughts jumbled through his brain, but by the time he had decided that he better run after her, if only to get the address, there was no sight of her in the crowded street.

11

Hal's spirits sank to their lowest ebb since he had left home all those weeks before. Why had he come to this daunting land so far from his roots? He had managed, by his own stupidity, to lose the one companion he had in this country. Now to cap it all the temperature seemed to be dropping rapidly and a few flakes of snow drifted slowly down from the dark sky above. He had to find a bed for the night, there was no possibility of sleeping on a bench in this weather, even if it meant spending some of his dwindling money reserves. He had to sort himself out and decide what he was going to do.

He wandered aimlessly on up the street until he noticed a sign advertising rooms. He went in and was shown into a large dormitory of bunk beds, reminding him of the accommodation in the S.S.*England*. Just like the ship, it was partly occupied by a mixture of men of varying appearance and nationality. At least it was out of the cold. He lay down on his back, hands behind his head, on the dirty mattress which he soon decided was already home to a hungry family of biting insects, but it would have to do for one night.

"Right Hal, me boy," he thought to himself. "You have several options you can take.

One - you could go to the newspaper office tomorrow, eat humble pie and find Maggie hopefully and start again with whatever Mr Baumgarten can come up with. That's if Maggie will have you back as a friend, of course.

Two – you could try and find work here in this city yourself, and possibly try and find Maggie, but how could you do that with only the one possible contact?

Three – you could move on and start again in some other city or part of this vast country. There must be many challenges out there."

The more he thought about this third idea the more it seemed to appeal to him.

He resolved the next morning to move on. It was a pity about Maggie, but there were other fish in the sea and he was able to convince himself that he had carried out his death-bed promise to Jason. He would go to the railway station early in the morning and take the first train to somewhere. With these thoughts he drifted off into a deep sleep.

As accustomed he woke early, once again feeling positive about the adventure unfolding ahead of him. He was able to get directions for the train station as he ate a sugary bun with his cup of tea.

The station was an impressive building, very similar to the great stations in London Hal had passed through on his way to Liverpool. A towering arched roof shrouded in a permanent mist of smoke from the steam engines. Once again at the sight and sound of the steam engines Hal's excitement increased and he immediately forgot his doubts of the previous night. This was the right thing to be doing. His attention was drawn to an advertising sign on the wall in large print.

"ENGINEERS AND OTHER TRADES WANTED FOR THE NEW 'NICKEL PLATE' RAILROAD. OPENING ON OCTOBER 22nd 1882.
APPLY TO THE SENEY SYNDICATE AT THE METROPOLITAN NATIONAL BANK OFFICES."

Hal could not believe his luck. This sounded like a heaven-sent opportunity. Here he was in the right place at not far off the right time. Surely they would not have filled all the positions by now; it was little more than a month since the opening of this new railway. Anyway it was well worth a try. If they would not accept him then he could still move west to another area.

There was no time like the present, so the same morning Hal presented himself at the 'Enquiries' desk of the bank. He was directed by the 'starched', black-suited, wing-collared clerk to take a seat to await an interview with a Mr Brice Junior, who was the New York representative for the 'New York, Chicago and St Louis' Railway. Hal did as indicated and nervously sat on the edge of the seat. He felt very overawed and definitely underdressed in this smart banking house where conversations seemed to be conducted in whispers and everybody wore tailed suits and grey cravats, not the scruffy old suit he had been travelling in for so long. His bed companions of last night also seemed to be having a late breakfast, as he scratched his leg.

Time seemed to drag by as he kept glancing up at the clock. Eventually after three-quarters of an hour he was approached by a young lad of probably no more than fifteen or sixteen, also dressed in a tailcoat.

"Please Sir, Mr Brice will see you now. Please follow me." Hal had never in his life been addressed as 'Sir'. It made him feel even more nervous than he had already been feeling during his wait.

He did as requested and followed the lad down a long passage with pictures of elderly gentlemen lining the walls. Underfoot a deep pile maroon carpet deadened their steps. At the far end the lad opened a door, stood back and invited Hal to enter.

All sorts of sayings flashed through Hal's mind. "In for a penny in for a pound." "Nothing ventured nothing gained." He was reminded of his mother who had been a great one for quotations to fit the moment. He said a quick mental prayer, asking for help from her.

As he stepped over the threshold he saw what appeared to be an empty room; walls wood-panelled, with leather bound books shelved at one end, a table covered in an untidy pile of papers, and the corner view of a desk peeping round the door.

Hal had expected to be seeing some crusty old gentleman; so was taken aback to find a young man of his own age sitting behind the large oak desk. He looked up, brushing an unruly lock of blond hair out of his eyes.

"Come in, Mr…" he glanced down at a piece of paper on his desk. "Slater," he said with a brief hesitation. "You are here as a result of our advertisement, I believe."

"That's right, Sir." Hal felt he was about to stutter as he stood in front of the desk, with his hat in his hands clasped in front of him.

"I was at the train station. I was wondering if you had already filled all the positions?"

"Tell me why you think you might be suitable for employment with us. Have you any skills?" he was asked pleasantly.

"Well Sir, to be honest I have no trade, but I have always been very good with machinery on the farm and have a great interest in steam engines. I can turn my hand to anything and certainly don't mind hard work."

"I see. So you are from an agricultural background? I would guess from England. When did you arrive in New York?"

"Just yesterday morning, Sir."

Hal thought that any chance he might have had would have gone. This smart young man obviously felt he was just some country boy come over on the boat. He might just as well plunge in with both feet now he was here.

"I had my own farm in Devon, Sir. I took it over when my father died and have now passed it on to my sister and her husband. I wanted to start a new life in engineering and thought that there would be opportunities here in America."

"Take a seat, Mr Slater. To be quite honest with you, we have already filled all the positions at the moment."

He stopped and looked down at the papers on the desk and thought for a moment before glancing up once more.

| ELEVEN

"What do you know about our Company, Mr Slater?"

"Nothing at all, Sir, other than what was on the hoarding at the station."

"Let me tell you then. We are a newly formed syndicate of bankers and businessmen who got together, under the chairmanship of my father, to invest in the railway business. We feel there are great opportunities for money to be made in developing the railway system in the North and Midwest. At the moment two men have a near monopoly of the railways – Mr Vanderbilt and Mr Gould. We want to get a finger in the pie as well," he said with a shadow of a smile as he brushed his wayward lock of hair back again. "Anyway, that's not your worry. We have bought the concessions and surveyed a route between New York, Buffalo, Chicago, and down to St. Louis. As you noted on the hoarding we have now built the track through to Chicago and ran our first train, the 513 miles through, a month ago. We are called 'The New York, Chicago and St Louis Railroad' or becoming known as the 'Nickel Plate Road'. That's the brief history lesson over for today!" Again that hint of a smile and the touching of his hair.

"Well, Mr Slater, what shall we do with you? I like the look of you. You have been honest with me I think. You have not tried to make yourself out to be something you are not. You appear a positive sounding sort of guy, the sort of young enthusiastic person I am looking for to help us expand this Company. What do you think if I offer you a job?"

"Oh thank you very much, Sir. If I might ask, what sort of a job would that be?... Please don't get me wrong, I am quite happy to do anything... Yes please, I would like the job" he added quickly.

"What I am going to do is give you a note for our Mr Stanovski in Buffalo, which is the rail headquarters, and he will find you suitable employment. Don't be disappointed if it's not the top job, you have plenty of time to advance in the Company if you have the will and ability. My impression is that in a few years we will be meeting again in a management capacity. I may be wrong, but that is up to you. If you work hard, then there are great possibilities in this new venture."

He drew some notepaper from a drawer and wrote for a few minutes, sealed it and passed it over to Hal.

"Take this and find Mr Stanovski in Buffalo. Now this is a rail pass to get you there as an employee of the Company."

"Thank you very much, Sir. I am very grateful for the trust you are showing in me. I will not let you down."

"For heaven's sake stop calling me Sir, it makes me feel old. I am Robert Brice junior. By the way what is your first name?"

"They call me Hal, Sir... Robert." He turned to the door to leave.

"By the way, Hal, have you got any money? You do look as if you had just come off a boat," he said with a chuckle. He put his hand in his pocket and pulled out a roll of notes.

"Here, take this to tide you over." He pulled a $50 bill off the top of the bundle. Waved away Hal's thanks. "See you around, Hal. Good luck!"

As Hal left the office Robert Brice junior's head went down to studying his papers once again as he pushed his hair back out of his eyes.

Hal got out on the street, glanced around and decided that now the world looked a better place. With the $50 bill in his pocket and a job he felt like a man of means again. His depression of yesterday was forgotten and he was on the verge of a new career. He just could not believe his luck. Eventually he found a men's outfitter that would not overstretch his new-found wealth. Half an hour later he emerged in a smart dark suit with a straw boater perched jauntily on his head and the other accoutrements a 'gentleman' might need, and having been assured that it was the fashionable outfit for an aspiring young man to be wearing this year. He returned to the station to check out the train times for Buffalo; he glanced up at the advertisement hoarding he had seen earlier in the day and tipped his hat to it with a silent prayer of thanks.

Rather than waste a day of his new-found life he caught the overnight train. It would also save having to pay for a bed if he did not delay his departure till the next day. It appeared to be a slow train, stopping at what seemed like every station along the way, but very soon this did not concern Hal as he dropped off into a deep sleep, lulled by the clatter of the wheels.

The train drew into Buffalo early the next morning. Hal reckoned that he would have to wait for a couple of hours before he approached Mr Stanovski. He 'sloshed' his face well in a basin in the toilets before getting himself a bun and coffee at a stall on the station. Coffee was not a beverage he had ever tried until two days ago, but he decided it was a pleasant drink with which to start the day; anyway, there did not seem to be tea available like there was at home.

Refreshed, he went to track down Mr Stanovski at the NY.C & St.L. Railroad office on an upper floor of the station. His knock on the door was answered by a female voice shouting at him to stop hanging about and just come in.

"Shut the door, it's a real cold morning today. I never put on my thick drawers this morning and the draft is fair whistling up my skirts. I will be with you in a moment."

The Irish brogue made him think guiltily of Maggie. He had really not treated her very well. I wonder what she is doing? Has she found work with her Mr Baumgarten? He realised with a twinge of conscience that in the excitement of his new job he had really not thought about her.

| ELEVEN

His speculation was brought to a stop as the woman turned towards him.

"Oh I am sorry, excuse me. I thought you were someone else coming in this early; we don't usually get visitors at this time of day. What can we do for you?"

The blonde-haired woman was well built, her narrow waist showing off broad hips from which hung a long black skirt; above, an embroidered white blouse buttoned tight to her neck. Hal, with 'all his experience' of women thought she was probably in her early thirties. She blushed at the thought of what she had said to this handsome young man.

"I have a letter of introduction to Mr Stanovski from Mr Robert Brice in New York. It's about a job," Hal added as an afterthought.

"Well, you must be the one he telegraphed about yesterday. You have not wasted much time, have you? Mr Stanovski is not in the office as yet. Perhaps you wish to wait. There's a chair there behind the door."

"Thank you. Yes, I will." Hal sat with his boater clutched nervously on his knees. He was not sure whether he should try and continue the conversation with the young woman. The decision was made for him as she turned back to go on with whatever she had been doing when Hal had entered.

Twenty minutes later the door burst open, banging against Hal's foot as it flew back.

"How are you this fresh morning, my little dove?" the tall man in the tailcoat asked of the young woman, quite unaware of Hal sitting behind the door. Hal could see her making frantic signs to the man as she turned to indicate that they were not alone. He spun on his heel towards Hal.

"Hello, what are you doing hiding away there?" quite unabashed at what he had said before.

Hal guessed he was Mr Stanovski by his thick accent. It fitted his name. His first impression of his height had been correct. He was well over six foot, slim, with a narrow lined face. About fifty years of age.

"I am Hal Slater. I have been sent to see you by Mr Brice."

"We had the telegraph yesterday afternoon about Mr Slater, you may remember, Mr Stanovski."

"Oh yes. Another boy wonder sent on to us to try and make something of. Although you do look rather more presentable than some of them. Come into my office and tell me what you are expecting to do."

He turned abruptly. Without waiting for Hal he shoved his office door open with a bang. Hal's immediate thought was that doors would not last very long with this man. What would he be like as a boss?

"I am quite prepared to do whatever work you have available" Hal stammered as he caught the door when it flew back again.

75

"Well, that's something. Most of them come in here thinking they should be Managing Director. What skills do you have? Don't try and pull the wool over my eyes as I will very quickly find you out if it's not the truth."

Hal took an immediate liking to this man; he seemed to call a spade a spade. He reminded Hal of Stephen, his father, in the happier days before he had become depressed by George's downfall.

"I am a farmer by trade, but have a very good way with machinery and a great interest in steam. As I said, I will do anything."

"Well, we do not have a great demand for farmers in the rail business, but having said that we are beginning to develop the carriage of cattle from the Mid West into New York. Perhaps your farming experience would be useful up in Chicago. I could do with a bright young man up there, talking to the dealers at the cattle yards."

This was not exactly the sort of thing Hal had had in mind, but he had said he was willing to try anything.

"Get yourself up to Chicago as soon as possible. Start talking to people at the Stock Yards. See if you can get an interview with Guy Balstrude; he is the buyer for the Armour Meat Packing Company. We need the freight business. Find yourself an office. Telegraph us here as soon as you get yourself set up. Money you can draw on our Chicago account, up to a certain limit. They will let you know how much when you see them. Talk to Maureen about all the details..."

"Sir."

Hal felt he just had to interrupt this flow of information, which he was trying to absorb, as it rattled out in a machine-gun like fashion as the thoughts chased each other out of Mr Stanovski's head in a non-stop stream. Mr Stanovski paused, probably only to draw breath and looked at Hal quizzically.

"What? Don't you want the job then?" His eyebrows, which were very dark and bushy, seemed to rise half way up his forehead.

"Yes Sir I do, but what is the job you are wanting me to start? I have a lot of experience with cattle, but know nothing of railroads..."

"I thought I made that clear. You will be the representative for the railroad at the Stock Yard. Now I have to go to a meeting. Anything else you need to know, just ask Maureen. She's the one who really runs this place!"

He picked up a bundle of papers from his desk and disappeared out of the office door like a whirlwind in the same fashion he had entered a few minutes before.

Hal went through to the outer office where he found the blonde, Maureen, standing at her desk with a broad smile on her face and laughing silently.

"My goodness, is he always like that?" Hal asked, still feeling mesmerised by the fact that he had got a job so easily, but really had not a clue what the job entailed.

"You will get used to him after a bit. He likes to leave things to people's initiative to do a job in the way they think best. If you are successful he will support you all the way, but show lack of initiative or laziness and you will be out on your ear before you can say 'begorrah'. Just remember that and you will get on fine. Now, what do you need to know?" she said with a twinkle.

"Well, everything!" Hal smiled back. He decided that Maureen would be very easy to get on with and would be the key to him making a success of what seemed like a daunting task ahead.

"I think a nice cup of coffee is the first thing to organise. Coffee is what makes the world go round in the good ol' United States. Then I will give you as much information and names as I can."

So began his first morning's work for NY.C & St.L Railroad with an intensive two hours of fact-finding. Hal scribbled as much as he could down on paper. Finally Maureen stopped talking.

"Now Hal, I have told you as much as I can think of at the moment, and I really must get on with the day's work. When you have settled yourself in, telegraph me the address and then, if I can be of more help, we will be able to communicate. Off you go, and good luck."

This was almost more than Hal could get his mind round. Three days ago he had been a nearly penniless immigrant arriving in a strange country with no job. Now he had become a citizen of that country, travelled well into the heart of it, been accepted as a trustworthy person by previously unknown people, landed a job of which he had very little idea what it was all about… Phew…whatever next?! Was this the way things always happened over here? This was not the way life had been conducted in rural Devon. He was used to the slow changing of the seasons with the routine round of work that went with each one. Anyway, it was no good hanging about here. He had to move on to Chicago and accept the challenge that had been set him.

CHICAGO AND THE STOCK YARDS

12

As the train trundled its way westward towards Chicago, Hal as always was fascinated by the changing scenery. Often with glimpses out over the vastness of Lake Eyrie; soon even this view was obscured by a change in the weather as the wind picked up and brought with it the first blizzard of the winter. Hal wondered, from the comparative warmth of the carriage, what it would be like to be on the open footplate of the engine. From time to time as the train rounded a sharper bend he was able to catch a glimpse of the engine with a cloud of smoke being dragged horizontally from its high funnel, only to be torn and broken by the wind.

At Cleveland they had a long enough stop to allow those passengers who wished to descend to stretch their legs on the platform. Not many took advantage of this exercise in the biting wind. Hal walked briskly up and down; after a while he was joined by a fellow traveller.

"Cold, isn't it," he remarked. "This is what we can expect from now on until Spring arrives and then shortly after that we will all be complaining about the heat. Are you stopping at Chicago or going on down to St Louis ?"

"I will be stopping at Chicago. I am starting a new job there. I work for the Railroad Company," Hal added proudly, as if he had been an employee for years rather than for one day.

"Oh yes. What job is that then?" the stranger enquired, in a rather disinterested voice.

"I am the Company representative to build up the freight trade from the Cattle Yards, shipping cattle and carcasses back east." Hal hoped he would not ask much more as he felt on very unsafe ground regards his new position. The last thing he wanted was to be made to look foolish.

| TWELVE

"Oh yes," his new companion replied disinterestedly. "I'm in gents' clothing. Fit you up with whatever you need. I usually work in and around New York, but my Company want me to expand into the Middle West."

Hal was relieved to get away from this cocky boring stranger, as the engine's whistle let out two piercing blasts, and the hardy souls on the platform hurried to get back to their seats and into the warmth of the carriages.

By late afternoon the journey had begun to seem interminable. Would they ever get there? Even Hal's enthusiasm for trains was beginning to wane. Now he was keen to meet the challenge of his new job. He had seen enough of snow-covered countryside. He had dozed in his seat. He had tried to make polite conversation with his fellow travellers. He felt full of frustrated energy. He needed to be at some manual task. All in all he was bored; not something he had ever had time for in his previous life.

After dark they reached a city sprinkled with dim flickering gaslights. Hal decided that this must be Chicago, judging by its size. At last they started to rattle over junctions, as other lines joined their own, and finally pulled into the terminus.

In spite of his inactive day Hal felt quite ready for a good night's sleep. So the first thing was to find comfortable lodgings for this night at least, tomorrow he could find something more permanent out near the Cattle Yards. An enquiry soon led him to a small hotel. As he was a man of some 'importance' he could not go to some doss house as before, anyway he had some funds now.

He enquired the next morning, from the hotel reception desk, the best way to get himself to the Stockyards.

"You mean the 'Union Stockyards and Transit Company', I expect, down at 'Packingtown'?"

"Well, it sounds rather silly but I really have no idea where it is or what it is called. I was just told to get there. Is there more than one Yard?"

He was very reluctant to add to his apparent ignorance by admitting that he had just been given an important job there. Why on earth had he not found out more from Maureen. She had said it was to the south of Chicago. Perhaps she did not really know, after all her job was in the Buffalo office.

"Union is the biggest by far, but there are others as well. Union is down south of the city. If that's where you want to go, then go out of here, turn right, and walk three blocks down to Michigan Avenue, take another right and you will see the tram stop marked 'Packingtown'. I don't know how often the tram goes, or you could walk down over the Canal and ask the way."

"Thanks for your help. I will go on out to the stop and see when they run, if there is not one for a while I will walk. How far would it be?"

"Oh, I guess I don't really know. I have never been down that far. Wouldn't be more than five mile, I suppose."

Hal reckoned that he could probably walk there as quickly as the horse tram would make it, so set off as he had been directed.

After an hour he knew he was getting close as he could hear the lowing of hundreds of cattle and the 'delicious' smell of cow manure wafting towards him on the gentle breeze. A lump came to his throat as these senses brought back his memories of his life at Cogwell Barton. This was all very exciting but he did miss the quiet rural life of changing seasons. What was he really doing in this place, starting a job he knew nothing of, and certainly not the sort of job in the countryside he had planned? Somehow the city was all bustle and rush, noisy and dirty.

He realised with a guilty conscience that he had made no effort to write to his dear sister Sarah to tell her that he was safely arrived in America. This made him feel even more lonely and without a friend in this sprawling city. What if he were knocked down in the street or got in a fight in some tavern; no one would know who he was or where he had come from. This led him to think of Maggie. He should never have run out on her- but then if he hadn't he would not be here at the start of his new career, but he did miss her. Not just as a friend, but as something much deeper.

He rounded a corner and he was there.

He did not quite know what he had been expecting, but it was not what was before his eyes.

There across the street was the most imposing gateway he had ever seen. It was enormous! A buff-coloured limestone archway with substantial gatehouses to each side. The centre of the archway had a high pitched roof which glowed a dull green in the morning light. However, the eye was immediately drawn to the centre of the arch, which was dominated by a carved stone bull's head, fully equipped with great spreading horns. It was most impressive.

Hal wound his way through the mass of traffic: people, horses and wagons coming and going busily along the street and through the imposing gateway. Once inside it was like another town. Hotels, restaurants, shops, and offices lined the road leading on further to row upon row of pens. Some with overhead walk or droveways leading down to other roads. Boardwalks ran down each pair of lines of pens to enable safe viewing of the stock.

As Hal got further down the main thoroughfare he could see that to each side of the vast area were railroads packed with box cars and open stock cars. Away, in what seemed like the distance, were more buildings, many with steam and smoke puffing out of tall chimneys. He almost felt he was walking along with his mouth open in amazement; never had he imagined that anything like this existed. He realised that everything in this vast country seemed to be on a grand scale, but this was beyond belief. These yards must cover an area many times the area of Cogwell Barton, the whole farm; come to that the whole of Squire Barraclough's Swinsbeck Estate. Now he was to be a part of it.

Maureen, in the Buffalo office, had given him a short list of names that should be good contacts to make. They were a mix of slaughterhouse buyers, stock agents, and packaging factory salesmen. First though he had to establish a base and make contact with the N.Y. & St.Louis's bankers. He quickly decided this was the first thing he should do, as he would need funds to rent an office.

Michigan State Bank, along with many others, had a branch within the Yards.

Hal straightened his boater, pulled his topcoat straight and marched purposefully in at the door and up to the clerk.

"I am Hal Slater of the New York and St. Louis Railroad. I would like to see the manager, if you please." Hal said importantly but feeling rather nervous.

"Please take a seat. I will see if he is available at this time." He returned a moment later. "Follow me, if you please, Sir. Mr Svenson will see you now." He led the way down a short passage and knocked lightly on an office door, opened it without waiting for a reply and announced. "Mr Slater, Sir."

Hal entered removing his boater. Coming round from behind a large desk, with his hand extended, was a broad-shouldered, very well built man with shoulder length blond hair in his early fifties. To Hal he looked more as if he should have been a lumberjack rather than a bank manager.

"Mr Slater, pleased to meet you. I was expecting you as we were telegraphed from your Buffalo office." He gripped Hal's hand in a crushing handshake, which Hal returned equally strongly. Hal guessed from his name that he was of Scandinavian extraction and his accent confirmed this.

"Glad to make your acquaintance, Mr Svenson," Hal said confidently.

"Please have a seat. What can I do for you?"

"As you will have been informed, I have been appointed the Railroad representative in Chicago," Hal said with conviction. His ego was rising by the second as he got into the swing of being such an important person. "I will be needing to draw funds on the Railroad account from time to time to finance deals and things." He realised he was getting into deep water as he did not have a clue what he was talking about.

"Yes, I understand that. Buffalo has given me instructions that you can draw $50 a week for expenses. Anything over this amount you will have to have authority from them," he explained with a kindly smile. "Let me give you some advice, Hal. Is it alright if I call you by your given name?" he continued without waiting for a reply. "There are a lot of sharks operating in the Yards; you will have to be on your guard all the time, but I am sure you will quickly find your way around. I might add that it sounds as if you impressed Mr Brice junior and Mr Stanovski. They sound as if they have a lot of confidence in your ability to do a good job here. As you will soon realise, although the Yards have only been going for less than twenty years they are growing at an enormous pace. In just the last year alone they have taken in another 25 acres of land. The railroads are the lifeline of this giant hub that is the Yards, both for bringing in stock for slaughter and for dispatching the meat and products over the country. I am sorry I am beginning to lecture you!"

Hal quickly came to realise that this was a man who could be of great help to him in getting established.

"Thank you, Sir. I think I may well be coming to you regularly to get advice while I find my way around."

"Now, let me see about those funds you need," he said with a twinkle in his eye as he rang a small bell to summon his clerk. "You will need an office. Try Mr Johnson, four doors down to the right. He will be able to fix you up with a room. Do you have lodgings? Most important to be comfortable. Try Mrs Schmit in Pershing Road. Number 62 if I remember rightly. Her rooms are clean and not too highly priced. Here you are then, $50 cash, please just sign here where I have marked."

"Thank you, Sir. You have been a great help. I am very pleased to have made your acquaintance."

"Glad to have done business with you. I am sure you know, but you should keep receipts of any monies you spend. Oh yes I nearly forgot. An account has been opened in your name. Your salary and commission will be paid direct into it for you to draw on. Once you are settled in you must visit one evening and have dinner to meet my wife and family."

"That would be most pleasant. Goodbye for now Mr Svenson."

Everything was happening almost too fast for Hal to take in. Information about an office, lodgings, and his salary. Good lord, he realised, he had never discussed this, or even thought about it, in the excitement of meeting Mr Brice, and he had not had a chance with the tornado-like Mr Stanovski. Then Mr Svenson had mentioned about commission. What on earth would that be? It would look really daft to go back and ask. Better to just wait and see what appeared in his new account.

13

Hal came out of the bank in a daze, automatically turned right without thinking and found himself four doors down standing in front of a rather tatty door. "Pull yourself together Hal, you have to go to work," he said to himself. He rapped on the door and entered into a narrow passageway. The door to the left was open, with the sound of voices coming from it.

"Yes Sir, can I help you." The black lad of about sixteen had turned, as Hal had entered, stopping his conversation with the young woman behind an untidy desk.

"Thank you. I am looking for Mr Johnson. I wish to talk to him about renting office space. Is he busy?"

"No, he is not busy at present," the lad replied with a smile. "How large an office are you looking for? Do you require one or two rooms, or more?"

"I think I would rather discuss that with Mr Johnson, if you please," Hal replied severely.

"I am Mr Johnson, actually!" The smile developed into a chuckle as Hal's face registered a total look of surprise and embarrassment.

"You are Mr Johnson? Oh, I am sorry, I was expecting someone slightly older-looking." Hal began to flounder, but was saved from further embarrassment as 'the lad' put on a pair of wire-rimmed glasses.

"There, does that help? You are not the first to be caught out, thinking they were talking to the office boy! And you did not expect a black to be running a business. If we had been down south that could not have happened. Now, down to business."

Hal stuck out his hand. "Hal Slater. I have just arrived to start as the agent for the New York Chicago & St.Louis Railroad. I need a small office to establish a base initially. Later, depending on business, I might need to expand. I wonder what you have to offer?"

"Let's start again. I am Joel Johnson." The smile returned as he shook Hal's hand warmly. "Well, two rooms spring to my mind quickly. Yes, let me think.

I believe that one would suit you perfectly. It is quite near to the N.Y.C & L track. Would you like to go over and have a look now?"

Once again Hal had been taken by surprise. He had never spoken to a black man before . In fact had seen very few, and those only in Liverpool at the start of his journey. They were a rarity in Devon.

"I am intrigued by you, Joel. Excuse me being blunt, but were you born in Chicago, or did you move north with your family?" he asked as they walked together across the Yards between the pens filled with all manner of stock. The noise here was quite something. A raucous hubbub of lowing, bleating, snorting all overlying the shouts and curses of the drovers.

"I don't mind at all you asking about my roots. In fact it is nice that you should be interested. A quick potted history of the Johnson family would be a pleasure. They lived in Virginia, near Richmond. You may know that this was the centre for much of the fighting during the Civil War. My parents and ancestors for generations going way back were slaves on a tobacco estate. When the war was finally over in '65 they were freed. This meant that they no longer 'belonged' to anyone and therefore had no employment. They moved north to here to find work. My father was here soon after the start of the Yards and worked here all his life. Almost from the moment I could walk I have run wild round the Yards, so know my way around fairish. I ran errands, delivered messages and letters and met a lot of people and knew exactly what was going on throughout. This led to being asked from time to time for information, until I decided to put it to good use and make a living from it. So there you are. The story of how one black boy has made good!" This time with a loud guffaw of laughter.

They soon arrived at a row of red brick two-storey buildings backing onto the rail tracks, but separated from the stock pens by a wide roadway full of the usual crowd of people and carts that seemed to be the norm for the Yards. At the end of this road were the factories with the tall chimneys Hal had seen from the other side of the Yards.

"Now this one will suit you well, I think. As you can see it is near the railroad. Your 'lot' are down at the end of the street. The processing plants are nearby. Perfect for your purpose, what more could you want?"

"Right, Joel, you are beginning to sell it to me! Let's have a look inside."

Joel produced a key as if from nowhere and opened the tatty door nearest to them. The paint was peeling off it, and the window frame next to it. As Joel pushed it open, with some difficulty, it scraped over the flagstone floor and a musty damp smell wafted out into their faces.

"Come in and have a look round," invited Joel with a lop-sided grin. "Don't be deceived by first appearances. You can quickly get this smartened up. I know just the person to slap a coat of paint on for you and get it tidied up."

THIRTEEN

From the entrance the short flagstoned hallway led straight on up to a wooden staircase curving round to the left and out of sight. At the bottom of the stairs a doorway gave access into a small room whose window looked out over the street.

"It all looks rather a mess, Joel. Not what I had been expecting. Also I only need the one room, I assume the stairs lead to another."

"Oh don't be put off, Hal. As I said it can be made OK with very little trouble. The room upstairs I can throw in for nothing until such time as you need to expand, which I am sure will be quite quickly once you get the business under way."

"What would the rent be? And who is the owner of the property?"

"I own it and the two on each side." Joel grinned at Hal's look of surprise. "I told you this was one black boy who had made good! The rent, now let me see. I think to a big rich organisation like yours it would have to be $2 a week. That's a very generous offer; I will hardly be covering my costs at that price."

Hal thought for a moment.

"Joel, you are a rogue! I know I am new to the Chicago Yards and have only just come off a ship. Back home in England I was a farmer and well used to making deals with folks like you. Mr Svenson warned me that you were a smart trader, and that you would try me out! I tell you what, I will pay you $1 a week, but first you must make this place presentable, the doors and windows fitting properly and painted inside and out. This room painted throughout; but we won't worry about the upstairs seeing you are not charging me for it! How does that sound? I shouldn't think your painter will cost much as I have a feeling it is you!"

"Hal, you are a hard man. Just like my old father described the slave masters. How can a black boy get on in the world with a rent of $1. Tell you what we will split the difference, make it $1.50 and I will tidy it for you. I must have a word with Mr Svenson. He is going to bankrupt me! Maybe I will move my account to someone else."

"Right, we have a deal. Put it there." They both spat on the palms of their hands and slapped them together. "I tell you what. Out of the goodness of my heart, just to help out the 'poor black boy' you get the paint, white I think, and I will paint out this room while you see to the rest. In the meantime where does a man go for a drink round here? I will buy you one to seal the deal."

The Yards were not short of drinking establishments and by the time Hal persuaded Joel to let him go to visit Mrs Schmit about his lodgings at 62 Pershing Road, he decided that he had better fill himself up with black coffee before he approached the lady for the first time. She might be a strong believer in temperance; it would not do to breathe fumes of liquor over her at their first meeting.

No. 62 Pershing Road was the complete opposite of the office space Hal had hired from Joel. The step was scrubbed, the paintwork immaculate, the brass door furniture shone in the sunshine with a brilliance that made Hal squint. He rapped firmly on the door with the knocker, hardly daring to touch it in case he should leave finger marks on it. He caught, out of the corner of his eye, the net curtains twitch in the window to the side of the door. A moment later the door opened.

"Come in, Mr Slater, I have been expecting you, but I had thought you might have been here earlier. Mr Svenson sent his clerk round to tell me he had recommended me to you."

Nothing seemed to be secret in this city. Everybody knew everyone else's business. On reflection Hal realised that it had been the same back home in Devon, but on a much smaller scale.

In front of him stood a diminutive woman of indeterminate age, but Hal guessed in her early seventies. Like the front of her house, her dress was immaculate. Woollen shawl draped over her birdlike shoulders, her boots, peeping out from under her long dress, shining as bright as the doorknocker. Her grey hair tied neatly up in a bun on the back of her head.

"Well, Mr Slater. Have you seen enough?" Hal realised he had been staring rudely. He could feel his cheeks reddening with embarrassment.

"Now let me tell you the house rules. You must be in by ten each evening, no strong liquor allowed in the house, no women in your room at any time, but you may entertain ladies in the lounge provided you have warned me first. You must be promptly on time for all meals which are breakfast and tea. Mealtimes are breakfast at seven, except on Sundays when it is at eight, tea at six. No smoking in the house anywhere; you must take your boots off as you come in. I do not return rent money if you have to be away, which I gather you may have to be from time to time. You may have one bath a week on Fridays; one week's notice of quitting. There, that will do for the time being. I have two other young men lodging with me. You will meet them at tea. My charge is $2 per week. How does that sound to you?"

Hal felt quite taken aback. It sounded as if there was no option but to take the room.

"That all seems very good," he stammered. "May I just see the room, please?"

"Of course, I am surprised you had not asked that at the beginning." As she turned, Hal smiled wryly to himself. There had not been one moment since the door was opened when he could possibly have spoken.

She scuttled up the stairs ahead of him, at a ferocious speed, to the second floor, threw open one of three doors on the top landing.

"There you are. Mr Mankowvich is in that one and Mr Guiesepsi is in there." She shut the door and was away down the stairs.

Hal had just had time to see that the room contained a bed, wardrobe, chest of drawers, and a small writing table. The wood floor had a small woven mat at the foot of the bed.

She held the front door open for him as he caught up with her.

"When do you wish to move in, Mr Slater?" There was no question in her mind apparently that it was not taken for granted that he would become her lodger.

"May I collect my bag from Mr Svenson's office and come straight back?"

Hal thought he would spend the rest of the afternoon familiarising himself with the Yards and try to get an idea of where the various offices of his contacts were situated. He found his way in again from Pershing Road.

Just outside the impressive limestone main gate was a painted wooden notice board.

UNION STOCKYARDS & TRANSIT COMPANY
OPENED IN 1865
WE FEED THE NATION.

As he stepped through the gateway, he was once again impressed by the size of the stock penning in front of him. His only experience of markets had been his trips to Honiton when he had needed to sell a beast. There the cattle had been tied to the railings in the main street, having been driven there by the drovers who had collected them from the farm. While the sheep and pigs were penned at the bottom of Silver Street, they had arrived in carts, although at the autumn sheep fairs they too were driven.

This was something again. There was continual movement of beasts. Some being unloaded from rail wagons and penned; while others, even at this time of the afternoon, were being herded off towards the factory-like buildings, he presumed for slaughter. The thought of this made Hal shudder; it was just the sheer numbers that must be involved.

He was not squeamish about the killing of animals for food. He had been brought up from the moment he could walk to the ritual of pig killing in the yard behind Cogwell Barton.

Not a drop of blood was wasted. Hal's father, Stephen, at each 'ceremony' had always pronounced that if they could have thought of a use for the squeal, they would have used it! He had probably learnt the 'joke' from his father and so on, back! With these thoughts came a wave of homesickness. How were Sarah and Richard faring at the Barton? What a lifetime away from this moment it seemed, another life.

Hal decided that the only way he was going to establish himself in his new task was to have some help to show him around. He knew just the man for the job! Joel.

He found his way back to Joel's office. The same woman was still behind the cluttered desk.

"Where am I likely to find Mr Johnson please?"

"He is out doing a job at present, Mr Slater. I don't know when to expect him back. I would guess that it won't be until tomorrow sometime," she replied with a smile. "He's busy with one of his properties," followed by a distinct giggle behind her hand.

Hal hoped that this did not indicate that he was going to have a problem with Joel over his new office deal. He would go straight round and have another look.

The outside of the red brick building looked much the same except the front door had disappeared. As Hal stood with hands on hips, mentally cursing to himself; a sudden burst of song erupted from inside, rising to a climax over the hiss of a sharp saw slicing through wood. He stepped quietly over the threshold to see Joel, with his back to him, busily working on the door, set up on a pair of trestles.

Hal stepped up behind him, and touched him on the shoulder.

"Glad to see my landlord is getting on with the job so speedily."

Joel physically 'jumped out of his skin', the singing stopping in mid-word, the saw falling from his hand with a clatter, his glasses nearly dropping from the end of his nose.

"Oh man. You do that one more time and my heart will stop. On second thoughts, it might be the last thing you do, I am renowned for my killer punch and instant reflexes!" This seemed very unlikely as Joel, apart from looking just a lad, was of a very slight build and only came up to the level of Hal's chest. They both dissolved into laughter.

"There's your paint or rather whitewash. I will be finished with my joinery by this evening so you can start your decoration tomorrow, move in the next day and be ready for business. I can arrange for a sign writer to make you a board to go outside. You will want a desk and chair, which I will get for you. Anything else you need just come to the office and let me know."

"Yes, that sounds very helpful Joel. There is one more thing you can do for me. That is to give me a day of your time to show me round the Yards and introduce me to the people I need to know. Can you do that?"

| THIRTEEN

"Sure. That's easy. Little ol' Joel knows everybody who is anybody round here! Do you want to do that before you cover yourself in whitewash, or after, Mr Limey?" he teased and doubled up with laughter at his own joke. "Whitewash... Mr Limey!" he was off again, eventually coming to a wheezing stop. "I should really be on the stage."

Hal could not help smiling at this exuberant young man. Gave him a hearty slap on the back and said.

"Tomorrow would suit me fine, and I will become 'the little ol' white boy' the day after." Hal tried to impersonate Joel's 'deep south' accent. It did not come out too well mixed with Hal's broad Devon dialect.

14

"OK Joel, let's get this conducted tour on the road."

"Right man, where do you want to start? The packing plants, slaughter lines, railroads? You name it, I will take you there. I knows everybody who is anybody round these parts."

"I think it best to start at the beginning. So we had better have a quick look at the animal transport into the Yards and what happens to them when they come in. Does that sound the right way to do it? Then we will move on to the slaughter lines etc."

So started a hectic non-stop day of looking at the operation of the Yards, talking to the people involved, and generally finding where everything was situated.

In spite of Joel's claims that he knew everybody, Hal soon realised that Joel operated only with the bottom half of the social scale. The more important bosses Hal would need to approach himself, and these were the ones he would need to do business with, but it was a start.

The stock and operation of the Yards were really of more interest to Hal than the people; being of a farming background and with his interest in machinery.

It seemed that the stock, which was practically all either cattle or hogs, as pigs were called over here, mainly arrived on rail wagons. The drovers' sole job was to drive animals from the wagons to penning and then, as required, on to the slaughterhouses. The drovers worked in gangs of three or four men, one of whom was always a clerk to keep note of what was put in which pen, how many in the batch, and where they would eventually be moved on to. There was food and water available in each pen to allow the beasts to recover after what could have been a long journey in a rail wagon, before they were taken for killing.

The animals' last walk was up inclined ramps onto the second or third floor of the slaughter house, so that as they were butchered gravity could be used to dispatch each part of the animal to its respective processing area.

| FOURTEEN

When they got to the slaughter line Hal felt rather sickened by the sheer numbers. He had spent his whole life at Cogwell in the tender caring of animals without really thinking too much about their ultimate end. That is not to say that he had been sickened by the annual pig kill, usually near Christmas time. It was a tradition going back for centuries. The hams and shoulders would be rubbed in salt, prior to being hung up the chimney to smoke. Brawn made in the moulds from the heads. The lard collected by rendering the fat down, and all the other pieces used, nothing was wasted. It was in the interest of farmers to look after their stock as if they were one of the 'family', and it was only right that at the end of their time they should help to feed the family.

Here the cattle seemed to be just something that was pole-axed as quickly and easily as possible before having their throats cut and allowed to bleed out as they hung on the beginning of the production line.

This line intrigued Hal with his mechanical mind. It was a long endless chain moving slowly and continuously round, onto which the freshly killed carcass was hung. As it moved along an army of butchers each did their allotted task. Cut and sawed at the body. First the hide was stripped off, followed by the head, then the entrails removed, next the feet and any other non-edible parts. These were all pushed down their respective chutes to be dealt with by other teams on the floors below. The hogs were treated in much the same way but rather than being skinned were scalded in boiling water prior to being scraped to remove the bristles. Finally the carcasses were split, given a very brief cursory inspection for health reasons, before being taken off the line and hooked on long rails in a building chilled nearly down to freezing. Here they would stay until completely cold.

Just like at Cogwell, no part of an animal was thrown aside.

By mid afternoon Hal had had enough of dead bodies and bits of animals. What could not be used for human consumption was processed into a great range of products from fertiliser, soap, the hides into leather, glues, gelatine, and numerous things he had never even heard of.

"Right Joel, I have had enough of this to keep me going for ever. What about the transport out of all these by-products and the meat itself? I have a list of companies and people I should be in touch with. Where are they? Here, have a look at this. Armour Meat Co., Morris Meat Co., Swift's."

"Yes Sir, that's no problem. You just follow me!" he said with his usual air of confidence. He set off down a road to the side of the slaughterhouses towards a large more office-like building.

"Now, there you are. The Armour Meat Company, and over there is Swift's." He seemed reluctant to go right up to the door. Hal sensed that this was one part of the Yards that Joel did not have access to. He could see that this was a good opportunity to make up for the bragging and self-importance that he had had to put up with all day. It would bring Joel down a peg and make up for the constant teasing.

"Come on then, Joel. Are you going to take me in and introduce me to the important people like you have been doing all day? These are the big wheels round here. The important people. The ones I really need to know. These people will be asking me over for dinner and to meet their beautiful daughters. You tell me you are friends with everybody on the yards, so come, what are we waiting for? I want to meet them." Hal set off to stride over to the entrance where a uniformed doorman stood.

"No, wait a minute Hal." Joel grabbed his arm. "You can't just go running in there like that. Them's not like us folk. They won't let you in there."

"What you mean is, they won't let you in there, isn't that right? I am the big wheel of the New York Chicago & St. Louis Railroad round here, so a very important person."

"You know nothing, Mr Hal. I am an important business man," he said stuffily, and then suddenly realised he had been set up. "But then I am also an office painter just like you, so that puts us on the same level." They slapped hands and laughed; turned away from the smart part of the Yards and went off to talk to some of the railroad men.

"Hal, this is Don, this is Mr Hal Slater, your new boss. He's really going to tan your ass, man!" Joel stepped smartly back as Don swung a dinner plate sized hand to cuff Joel round the ears.

"You cheeky little boy. One of these days I'll tan your ass so hard you won't be able to sit down for a month." He turned to Hal. "Pleased to meet you Mr Slater, I did hear tell that there was a new manager on the way. I'm the foreman here for our railroad. I look after all the loading and dispatch of the wagons, so I guess we will be working alongside each other a fair bit."

Don McKlaskey was a big man in all respects. Though of no great stature, probably only standing at 5 foot 8 inches, he appeared to be almost as broad and with tree trunk sized arms attached to his powerful shoulders. His coat jacket stretched tightly across as if the seams would burst open at any minute. Not the sort of man to get in a fight with, Hal thought as he put out his hand which was gripped firmly but not overpoweringly. He took an immediate liking to him.

"I am going to need a lot of guidance about this job until I get the hang of it and have met our customers. I hope I will be able to rely on you, Don, for that help."

"You can do that, Sir. I hear that this little pip-squeak here," taking another swing at Joel, "has set you up with an office. I had better come on over tomorrow and answer any questions you may have. If that's alright with you?"

| FOURTEEN

"Heh, Ha, you could use him to do the whitewashing, though I am not sure he has enough brain to be able to do that," Joel said as he dodged another swipe from Don by hiding behind Hal.

Hal reported for breakfast, at 62 Pershing Road, on the dot of seven the next morning, and was busy on the end of a paintbrush in his new office soon after. Don arrived mid-morning when the job was half done and Hal was quite ready for a break.

"Good morning Don, come on in and have a seat. Have a care, though I don't know what rubbish Joel might have passed off to me! It could easily collapse on you. He is a bit of a character though, have you known him long?"

"Oh he is a good sort in spite of his cheeky ways. We get on well together, really, in case you may have thought otherwise. He has done well for himself you know. He arrived here just as a scrap of a lad , not that he looks much more than that now, with nothing, but by sheer hard graft he has built up a useful business. If you want information then Joel is your man."

"Yes, I rather had that feeling. Now bring me up to date on what the Company is doing and with whom. Maureen back in Buffalo gave me an hour's briefing on the job, but other than that I am pretty vague about the important people and companies in Chicago. You know Mr Stanovski and his secretary Maureen, I suppose?"

"Mr Stanovski, yes. He is the one that has been my boss as it were. A hard man but fair. Leaves me alone to get on with it most of the time. The two main companies we are shipping for are Armour Meat Company and Swift's, and some for Morris. In the main it is carcass meat in barrels, boxed meat products, the new stuff they call Margarine, sacks of fertiliser made from meat blood and bones. Then there are the soaps and glue and lots of other by-products that come from several other companies as well. My team, I employ about 50 or 60, depending on how busy we are, load the box cars and dispatch them back east or down to St. Louis."

"That's very helpful, Don. It seems that I should make contact with the representatives of the companies first."

"There is one other thing that you should know. I have only heard it as a rumour so far, but it sounds sensible and is probably the way rail shipping of perishable things will have to go. Refrigeration… I hear that some ships, of certain shipping lines, have been doing it for about two years, so why not have refrigerated box cars?"

"Thanks. That is a useful sales pitch when I get to see our customers."

Hal made his first appointment with a Mr Stewart at Swift's. He quickly realised that it had been a good choice.

"Come in Mr Slater. I gather you are the agent for the New York, Chicago and St. Louis Railroad. Glad to meet you. As you know we do quite a lot of business with you. What can I do for you today?"

Mr Stewart seemed to Hal to be an open, welcoming sort of person. Hal's friendly cheerful looks and relaxed manner certainly made it easier for him to get his 'foot in the door' with people. He thought he would come straight to the point; after all being new to the job he had not much else to offer.

"We are most grateful for the business you give us, Mr Stewart. There is something I think we can help you with to extend both our businesses. I believe you are just thinking about refrigeration."

"I can't imagine where you have heard that," Mr Stewart replied quickly with a smile. After a moment's thought he continued, "actually you have heard correctly. We have had built several refrigerated boxcars. You are the first outside the Company we have discussed this with, so I would appreciate it if you did not make it public knowledge for the time being until we have them delivered next month. Then I will discuss with you a contract to run them with the other freight trains.

"No doubt our rival meat packing companies will have heard the rumours you have heard and will wish to discuss terms with you as well. There is no reason to think that it will not work successfully and enable us to transport our products all over the country using the connecting links of the railroads. Your Company as the 'local' railroad will benefit from being able to establish those links for us. It should be an enormous step forward in the transport of perishable products throughout the country and indeed throughout the world. The prospects for the export and import trade are unimaginable." They continued discussing business and more general matters for another half hour. Mr Stewart glanced at his pocket watch, thought for a moment, came to a decision and asked Hal. "Now I was just going to take a light luncheon at the club, would you care to join me? I think there is a lot more we should discuss and I would like to get to know you better."

"Thank you Sir, it would be my pleasure." Hal realised that this was a great opportunity to get to meet some more of the leading citizens of this city. And so it turned out to be. They descended to the street where Mr Stewart's carriage waited at the door. Hal just hoped that his one suit and neckerchief were suitable attire for the club, and that he did not still have the odd spot of whitewash in some unseen place on it.

The club proved to be as extravagant as it had sounded to Hal. A liveried black doorman took their hats before they moved through to the dining room, where the food was more sumptuous than Hal had ever had. Over coffee afterwards a portly gentleman approached them.

FOURTEEN

"Hello Stewart. Introduce me to your young guest. I don't think I have had the pleasure of meeting him as yet."

"Good day to you, Balustrade. I trust you have enjoyed your luncheon. Let me introduce Mr Slater of the N.Y&C Railroad. Hal, this is Guy Balustrade of the Armour Meat Company," he said turning to Hal with a wink.

"Pleased to meet you, Mr Slater. I had heard that the railroad had a new agent, but I had not expected to meet you here. Come and see me sometime." With that imperious order he turned on his heel and left.

"Don't be fooled by his manner, Hal. He's not a bad chap really, just rather full of his self-importance. I expect his feathers are slightly ruffled in that I had seen you before he had! I am sure he will want to talk to you about the little matter we were discussing before. He is bound to have heard, as I said to you earlier. One warning though, he likes to get his own way. He is not a man to get on the wrong side of."

Over the next few weeks Hal went round and met all of the companies who were customers of the railroad and many others as well. Gradually he began to feel more at home and confident in the job. He reported back to Maureen in Buffalo the progress he was able to make, particularly when the refrigerated boxcars arrived at Swift's. Immediately there was an upturn in enquiries from many companies wishing to keep up with their rivals.

15

Christmas and the New Year came and went. Mrs Schmit, at his lodgings in Pershing Road, gradually softened and started to treat him more like a son than the tenant he was. Spring poked its head up from the gloom of winter on more and more days. Hal, as his job became less daunting, found himself thinking back and wondering what had become of Maggie. By the middle of April he realised he had made an awful mistake. He should never have been so pigheaded and left her like that. Since arriving in Chicago he had hardly looked at another woman. There had not been time, but he came to the conclusion that subconsciously he had not wanted to and that he was deeply in love with Maggie.

At Mr Stanovski's next visit, a week later, Hal announced that he was going to take a week off to travel to New York.

"Yes, that's alright Hal. You have done well here since arriving and I know you have never had a day off. Go on and do whatever it is you need to do and come back refreshed."

This was almost the longest speech Hal had heard from his boss, and it took him by surprise. He had been expecting to have to make a very strong argument of his request.

He bought himself a new three-piece suit and bowler hat; withdrew money from his bank account; cleared up outstanding business and informed Mrs Schmit he would be away but would continue to pay the rent on his room. He wrote himself a rail pass, and two days later boarded the train for New York.

The journey east seemed interminable, but at last the train rolled into New York.

Hal had had plenty of time to consider his best way of tracking down Maggie. He realised that in a big city like this it could be an impossible task. He had no idea what work she could have found, even if she could easily have moved on to somewhere else. She might have decided to travel back to Ireland, though he thought that unlikely. She probably would not wish to see him after their last parting. She might have met someone else or, with all of his

| FIFTEEN

heart he hoped not, might even be married by now. He began to almost wish he had put her right out of his mind and had not started out on this foolhardy trip.

Then he mentally kicked himself as he realised that this was the stupid dithering that had caused him to leave her in the first place. Now he was here he would give it his best effort for the week he had available to find her. Even if it turned out badly, at least he would then know she was alright and he would have to put her out of his mind and start afresh.

If he could find that same bar where they had first stopped after arriving he might be able to track down the man they had spoken to about jobs. One thing Hal had always been good at was a retentive memory for places. He knew the area they had been in. That was where to start, and what better time than now.

After an hour searching and a couple of wrong choices he was pretty certain he had found the right place. He caught the barman's attention and ordered a small ale.

"I am looking for an Irish girl called Maggie O'Kelly. Dark hair, green eyes, about 5 foot 9 inches. I last saw her here about six months ago. I wondered if there is anyone of that description who comes in here?"

"Oh my friend, there are a lot of Irish girls who come in here with those sort of looks. I should like to find one as well."

"The other person I am looking for, who we met at the same time, may use this as his usual drinking place; he was grey haired, about 50, medium build, with an Eastern European accent. I think he had a night job with a newspaper, the *New York Herald* I believe."

"That one's easy, my friend. You must mean Frederick Baumgarten. Been coming here ever since I started the job. Comes in lunchtimes or early afternoon most days."

"Yes that's the name. I remember it now," Hal exclaimed excitedly. He pulled out his watch from his waistcoat. "Has he been in today?"

"I think you have missed him. Try tomorrow. Excuse me, I must serve these others."

Hal had time as he drank his ale to plan his next move. There was no harm in going to the *Herald* office and trying to track Mr Baumgarten down at work.

The Herald building was imposing. Stone steps leading up to large doors giving access to a lobby bustling with people. Hal approached the reception desk.

"I am looking for a Mr Frederick Baumgarten. I wonder if you are able to help me?"

The pretty girl behind the desk smiled up at Hal. "Oh I think that should be possible. Do you have an appointment?"

"No, no," Hal stuttered. He had not been expecting such a reply. 'Appointment' usually meant someone important; he had not put the man he had met in that category. Oh well, let's see who this is going to be. In for a penny in for a pound, as mother used to say.

"Go up the stairs over there to the third floor and enquire of his secretary if he will see you."

The third floor was grander than the second floor, which had been better than the ground floor. There was carpet on the floor and a prim-looking middle-aged lady behind the desk controlling the way through a door marked 'F.BAUMGARTEN. EDITOR.'

Oh, my goodness. Once again I have hit the top, thought Hal, thinking back to his job interview with Mr Brice junior.

"What can I do for you, young man?"

"I was hoping to see Mr Baumgarten for a minute. I have a very important question to ask him."

"What would that be, might I ask? This is a very busy time of day you know. A lot of people have very important questions to ask him."

"Well, it's personal."

"No, it won't be possible at this time. I can tell him if you leave a name and call back tomorrow…"

"Ethel. Has that copy come up yet from the news room?" The Editor's door had abruptly opened. There was the man from the bar standing in the doorway. He looked up and saw Hal. "Don't I know you, young man?"

"Yes Sir, we have met, six months ago in O'Rourk's bar on 23rd Street. I was with an Irish girl called Maggie O'Kelly. You said to come and see you about a job. I am looking for her and wondered if you could help." Hal came to a hesitant stop, realising what a silly request it was.

"Meet me in O'Rourk's at one o'clock tomorrow and tell me why you think I may be able to help you," he said abruptly and disappeared behind his door again.

Ethel shrugged and tut tutted. "There you are then, young man, you have your appointment."

Hal's immediate reaction was rather the same as it had been when he met Mr Baumgarten last time. His hackles bristled at the abrupt manner. Then as he made his way down the stairs, he calmed down and decided there was nothing to lose by being at the bar and meeting Mr Important Editor.

Twelve thirty and Hal was at O'Rourk's bar. He did not known what other chances he had of finding Maggie. Consequently he felt he had wasted the morning and was feeling depressed and not really holding out much hope that this meeting would achieve anything. On the other hand, why should Mr

| FIFTEEN

Baumgarten have agreed to see him? As the minutes ticked by he kept pulling out his watch nervously. He was into his third pot of ale by a quarter past one and no sign of Mr Baumgarten keeping the appointment. Hal decided that he would give him five more minutes, finish his ale and then leave. He looked at his watch a last time, banged his pot down and was getting to his feet when he felt a hand on his shoulder. He turned quickly, ready with a cross retort.

Standing behind him was a young woman. Her back was to the feeble light of the dirty window and in the smoky haze of the bar he was for a moment unable to make out her features. He peered closer. It couldn't be...

"Maggie?" he queried in a stuttering, shaky voice. "Is that really you?" as he got to his feet, knocking over the chair he had been sitting on.

"You must have had a pint or two of ale, Hal, if you are unable to recognise me after only a few months, and staggering around like a man in his drink. Maybe it would have been better if I had not been persuaded to come here."

Hal was rather taken aback; firstly that Maggie should appear as it were out of the blue, secondly that she should be scolding him. He took her arm to guide her to a seat, picking up his fallen chair, his fingers tingling at his touch.

"Oh Maggie. I was expecting Mr Baumgarten, you caught me by surprise."

Hal's eyes adjusted to the light and he could now see the old twinkle he had been remembering for the last few months, in those lovely green eyes. He realised that once again this fascinating woman was making fun of him. He loved it.

"Come here you big oaf. It's so good to see you." She embraced him with both arms in a lingering hug.

Cheers and laughter erupted from around the bar. "Come here, darling, and give me one like that. Why should he have all the fun."

"No boys. You don't deserve it like this one," she replied blushing deeply. She turned to Hal, straightening her short jacket with a nervous tug at the hem. "Let's get out of here and find somewhere quieter. We have so much catching up to do. I want to talk for ages, like we used to; hear what you have been doing." She stopped with a catch in her voice. Hal thought he could detect the glint of a tear on her cheek. His heart seemed to miss a beat, as he felt himself overflowing with emotion.

"Yes, there's a little park or green area just down the street with benches in it. I noticed it yesterday when I was hunting for this bar. Let's go there."

As they got into the street she took his arm. They neither of them said a word as they walked slowly down to the park. Both were too full of thoughts and bursting with emotion, not trusting themselves to speak, or knowing where to start.

"Here, this will do. Maggie how did..."

"What have you been…"

They both started together, stopped awkwardly, burst into happy laughter as they sat down and grasped their hands together looking into each other's eyes. They could both see there the longing and love for each other.

"You go first, Maggie. I must know how you came to find me in the bar, and then everything else you have been doing."

He still had a worried corner of his mind that she might have found someone else, but then her whole manner discounted that. All would be revealed soon enough. Just enjoy this happy meeting.

"Well, you remember back in November that Mr Baumgarten said to come and see him about a job. So the next morning, after you stormed off over our little disagreement…" She gave his hand a squeeze as he started to reply to that jibe, and he kept his mouth firmly shut. One thing he was going to definitely avoid was to have another jealous tiff with her.

"As you now know he is the Editor of the *Herald*. Well, there and then he offered me a job in the Bookkeeping Department. Of course I took it straight away; it saved me from going on the streets! I think he has kept an eye on my work as I have been promoted to second in charge now. Then yesterday he summoned me to his office. I thought that I must be in trouble, though for the life of me I could not think why. When I got there he said he had met a certain young man who had been enquiring about me. He would not say who it was and dismissed me brusquely saying that I should go to O'Rourk's today at soon after one o'clock if I wanted to see who it was, and that I could have the afternoon off if I wanted. That was all he said. Of course, as you know, I am of an inquisitive nature so could not resist coming to see who it was. I had no idea as of course, I know a lot of young men." She stopped for a moment to draw breath with the twinkle in her eye and cheeky expression that Hal remembered so well. "When I came in I could see your back which looked vaguely familiar. I thought that the 'carrot' top of hair looked rather like what I remembered yours looked like, but did not for a moment think it was you. I stood watching you for a moment, and then I knew when I saw your impatient banging down of your beer mug, and here I am. Now it's your turn."

Hal would have been quite happy for her to go on and on for ever, to have just listened and looked. He felt quite speechless.

"Come on, tell it all. I can't wait to hear what you have been doing. You obviously have done quite well for yourself judging by your dress. Certainly not sleeping rough on the streets."

So Hal went on to tell his story, with many interruptions from Maggie. Time flew by unnoticed until they suddenly realised the light was beginning to fade as the sun sank behind the buildings across the street. During the course

| FIFTEEN

of their long talk neither had made mention of friends of the opposite sex. Hal decided he just had to ask. He could not go on without knowing.

"Maggie, I have to ask. Is there anyone special in your life?" There, now it was out.

"Yes, there is, Hal. Someone I have fallen deeply in love with," she said without a glimmer of a smile.

Hal's heart sank to his boots. The elation of the last few hours together disappeared in a flash. How could fate be so cruel to him? The luck of meeting up again was all for nothing. He let go of her hand and looked down at the ground; feeling close to tears.

"Oh Hal, don't look so distraught. There is only one person, other than Jason of course, that I have loved. Surely you know… You… You great big ninny."

His head came up and a great smile spread across his face. His heart felt as if it would burst.

"Maggie O'Kelly, you once threatened to put this little farm boy over your knee and give him a good walloping. Now I think I will do just that to you. You are a cruel tease."

He took her round her slim waist and pulled her close to him as if to put her over his knee.

"Hal, please stop. You can't do that in public…"

Her protests were cut short as he gave her a firm lasting kiss on the lips.

At last, as they drew breathlessly apart, "Does that mean my dear that you feel the same?"

"Maggie I've been such a fool. Why did I miss the opportunity when it was there for us back when we first arrived here."

"Hal, do you love me like I love you?" She stamped her foot with impatience.

"Yes of course I do. I think I've loved you from the moment I first set eyes on you. Maggie, will you marry me and be my wife?" It was out now; he had said it without thinking.

"Hold your horses, that's a big step for a girl to be taking. I will need time to consider my answer, to be sure. What have you got to offer a simple Irish colleen?"

"Maggie, my heart. For once do stop messing about. I am not giving you time to think. Is the answer yes or no?"

"I've made my decision, I've had time to think… Oh yes please. How quickly can we arrange it? You can beat me every day so long as I can be your wife."

"Thank you, thank you. I will only beat you once a week, that will be enough I think; but I will love you for ever."

They embraced again. Hal wished this moment could go on for ever. Then he realised that by being married to Maggie, it would.

Eventually, as the chill of the evening increased and they were unable to keep it out by snuggling close together, Maggie reluctantly returned to her lodgings and Hal to his hotel, feeling as if he were in heaven he was so happy.

16

Maggie returned to work the next morning having agreed to try and make an appointment to see Mr Baumgarten as soon as possible. She would leave word with the girl at the front desk for Hal to be told what she had arranged. He had spent half the morning worrying that Maggie might have changed her mind, though in his heart he knew that she would never do such a thing.

"Is there a message for Mr Slater?"

The girl with the nice smile, he had seen yesterday, stood up, extended her hand: "Congratulations Mr Slater. I am so happy for you and Maggie. Yes, she said that Mr Baumgarten would meet you both at O'Rourk's at two. You are so lucky, you could not have chosen a nicer, kinder person."

"Thank you. I know I am the luckiest man in the world. How did you know I was to be congratulated?"

"Everybody here knows. In fact I should think she has told the whole of New York!"

He almost skipped out of the lobby and down the *Herald's* steps.

"Well, Hal Slater, what's this Maggie has told me? I feel responsible for her you know, as she has no one else in New York. Do you think you can provide for her? I suspect she has expensive ways."

This had been Mr Baumgarten's opening gambit as he had walked in with Maggie on his arm, as soon as he had shaken Hal's hand and while Hal and Maggie embraced nervously.

"Sir, she will just have to adjust to my low standard of living! I was a fool in more ways than one when last here. Apart from not asking her to marry me, I did not take up the offer of what might have been a good job in journalism! Not that I have regretted it as things have turned out quite well."

"You two men are talking about me as if I was of no consequence. Don't I get a chance to say anything?"

"No, except to tell me what you would like to drink to celebrate this happy occasion. I am delighted and honoured that you have involved me. No, on reflection, there is only one thing we can drink at this time. Barman ... A bottle of your best champagne."

Yesterday, during their long talk, Maggie had expressed the wish to ask Mr Baumgarten to give her away, which is why she had especially asked that he should meet them today. When their glasses were brimming with the bubbly golden liquid he turned to them, raising his glass.

"Congratulations. A very long and happy life together. Hal, look after her! In the few months I have known her, it has come to my attention that this is a very efficient and dedicated woman. As for you, I look forward to getting to know you. I have to admit that I have made a few enquiries about you this morning, once Maggie told me what you had been up to; I must say I have been impressed with what I have heard."

"Thank you, Sir. There is one thing that Maggie wishes to ask you. We had better let her have her say before she drinks too much of this excellent wine!"

"Mr Slater, I'll have you know that I could drink you under the table any day. We Irish girls are weaned onto alcohol, admittedly Guiness rather than this lovely stuff. I think I will get a liking for it! Now to be serious. Mr Baumgarten, Sir, would you do me the honour of giving me away on the special day of our wedding. You have been very good to me since we arrived in New York. My dear brother, Jason, is no longer with us, but if he were able to have a stand-in for himself, I know he would be more than pleased if you would do it."

"I would be delighted. I have no family or daughters to do this for, so consider it a great privilege to be asked. What's more, if you plan to have a bit of a party after the ceremony it shall be in the meeting room of the Herald if you wish. Now when is this all to take place?"

"As soon as possible, but I need time to plan my dress and things. Hal has to return to Chicago in two days' time and will not be able to leave his job again for a few months, so I think it is going to have to be in the autumn. I will have to give in my notice, too! Hal will have to find rooms for us in Chicago. There is an awful lot to plan. Now Hal, my love, I must get back to work. I don't want the boss giving me the sack!"

They met up for the next two evenings. The days seemed long for Hal trying to fill in the time. The following day he caught the train for the long journey back west. He stopped off in Buffalo to meet with Mr Stanovski and Maureen to discuss business and to express the hope that they would both join him in New York in the autumn.

Maggie and he had promised to write regularly to each other. Hal wished to be kept informed of the arrangements being made. He was leaving it all to

SIXTEEN

her as she was determined to have it just as she wanted. Hal was more than happy that it was happening and quite pleased to be leaving it all to her. The mention of writing reminded Hal that he had not written for several months to Sarah back at Cogwell, though she was a good correspondent writing regularly. How pleased for him she would be.

The leaves on the park trees began to turn a coppery brown as the first frosts of winter heralded in the autumn. October arrived and with it the time for Hal to make the long journey back east to his bride, accompanied by Joel who was to be his groom's man.

Maggie had quit her job and was able to meet him on the platform as the train drew into the station.

Two days later, in the early afternoon, they were wed at the small church one block away from the *Herald* offices. The party afterwards carried on well into the evening, hosted and generously paid for by Mr Baumgarten and attended by many of the friends Maggie had made through her work.

17

As they, this time together, travelled west at the start of their new life, Hal reflected on the lucky circumstances that had brought them to this point. His decision to give up his life in Devon; the chance meeting with Jason when he had chosen to bunk above Hal, leading to meeting Maggie. The selection of the bar that Mr Baumgarten used, and his job offer to Maggie. The chance that Hal had seen the advertising hoarding which lead to his meeting with Mr Brice. Life is certainly full of surprises which could go either way. In Hal's case, he was certain that he had dropped off on the right side of life's fence.

Hal, before he had gone east, had found a small furnished house to rent within easy walking distance of the Yards. It met with Maggie's approval and she soon put her mark on it with redecoration and her own nik-naks. Hal, with his many contacts, and with her glowing recommendation from the Editor of the *Herald*, found her a book-keeping job with Swifts.

So they settled into a happily married life of hard work and total contentment with each other. Hal's small circle of friends from his bachelor days, quickly enlarged as Maggie's personality worked its magic.

When in May Maggie announced she was pregnant, she was quickly taken under the wing of Mrs Schmit, Hal's old landlady, who like many had taken an especial motherly liking to her.

Sean arrived without due fuss or bother, followed at nearly annual intervals by Jason (named after Maggie's brother), Peter and Maureen.

"That's enough," Maggie exclaimed after a rather more difficult entry into the world by Maureen. "There's only so much a good Irish girl can put up with. Hal, you will have to hang your trousers somewhere else, not on the end of the bed!"

Maggie had given up her job at Swifts shortly before Sean's arrival. Hal took over Mr Stanovski's job when he retired. He now travelled much more with his new responsibilities; he did not like being away from his growing family. As the family grew they had moved into their own bigger house. Hal still ran his

| SEVENTEEN

business from the same office but now occupied the upper floor as well, much to Joel's pleasure. He was always reminding Hal that he had told him he would need it one day when he became an important person.

For some years Hal had felt frustrated that his job with the railroad was not leading anywhere. As other companies opened up new or competing routes, business became more and more competitive. In short, he was no longer enjoying his work as once he had done. His upbringing had been his simple life on the farm at Cogwell, and this is what he really missed, if he was honest with himself. The association with people who were close to and dependant on the reliability of nature. Then there was his long love of steam and farm machinery.

One of his business achievements had been to secure the contract made with the old well established firm of John Deere, manufacturers of ploughs, cultivators, corn-planters, wagons and sundry other implements based at Moline on the Mississippi river. Hal's contact in the company had been William Butterworth, a likeable go-ahead young member of the senior management. From the first meeting they had got on well together, discovering that they had many interests in common.

As 1890 arrived with penetrating cold, Hal and William met in Moline. Hal, feeling depressed, unloaded his frustrations onto William's attentive mind over a glass of wine.

"It sounds to me that you need to get back into farming, my friend. Why don't you leave the railroad and set yourself up with a nice little spread. Government lands are going cheap, especially if you know the right people."

"Huff, it's alright for you to talk, Willie. You have the right connections, not to mention that you are courting Katherine Deere. I have a wife and four children to provide for. I am sure that Maggie would have a fit if she thought I was throwing up my job to become a dirt farmer again."

"Well you could always join Deere's. We are constantly on the look out for people of your sort of calibre. You would then be back into agriculture at least."

The conversation moved on to other topics and Hal thought no more about it for some weeks.

The cold weather departed, blossom appeared on the trees, and Hal's thoughts turned once again to new beginnings. When next in the area of Moline he decided to make an overnight stop there rather than travel on to Kansas City. He hoped William would be available to meet him. William was now engaged to Katherine Deere, the daughter of Charles Deere the Company Managing Director. He sent word straight round from his hotel to William.

"This is so good to see you, Hal, but what a pity, I will be unable to meet you this evening. I am dining with Katherine and her parents," William explained when he returned the call having come round to Hal's hotel himself.

"Never mind, some other time." Hal replied, trying not to let the disappointment in his voice show.

"Hold on a minute, old boy. I have an idea. You have never met Katherine, have you? I am sure that you could join us for dinner if I ask tactfully. How does that sound?"

"I am not sure. I don't have a dress suit with me. I would hate to let you down by looking like something you had dragged off the street."

"No, that is no excuse. We are of much the same build; you can use my spare. Come on, we will go back to my rooms, send word to Kate, and give you a fitting."

The suit jacket was rather too short in the sleeves and the trousers came only to his ankles, but otherwise, considering his height not a bad fit.

"I don't really feel comfortable in this, Willie. I will feel embarrassed all evening and I don't want to let you down. What will Kate think of me?"

"Oh stop fussing, Hal. You are behaving like an old woman. Kate will love you and you will like her folks."

After much grumbling, their carriage drew up outside the Deere residence. A large solid house built in the Georgian style. The door was opened by a smartly dressed black servant who took their hats and coats before announcing them as he showed them into the drawing room.

Charles Deere crossed the room from where he had been standing with his back to the blazing fire in the big open fireplace.

He was of medium height, slim with mutton-chop whiskers down to his chin. He looked exactly the part of the rich successful businessman that he was, in his beautifully cut tailcoat and white tie.

"Come in, young sirs. Willie, introduce me to your friend."

"Yes Sir. This is my good friend Hal Slater who is the agent for the railroad in Chicago and west. Hal, this is Charles Deere."

"It is a pleasure to meet you Sir, and particularly kind of you and your wife to allow me to join you this evening."

"Now, Gabriel," he turned to the servant who had been waiting by the door, "a hot toddy for our guests if you please. They need warming on this cold evening." He turned back to Willie and Hal. "The ladies will I am sure be joining us very shortly."

"Now Hal, may I call you by your given name, we like to be informal here," he went on without waiting for a reply, "Willie tells me you are thinking of changing your career and you come from an agricultural background."

| SEVENTEEN

Hal glanced across to Willie, giving him a look that could have killed. He had not been expecting that Willie would have passed on their discussion of some weeks before. He certainly would not have come if he had known that it would be a job interview. He had not prepared himself for this and would not want word to get back to the railroad board.

"Well Sir," he blustered for a moment, not quite sure what direction to take, " I think possibly Willie has jumped the gun a bit... I had not given it much thought. However my interests from an early age have always been with farm machinery and steam engines, so I suppose, given the right opportunity, I would consider a change of career. I do have a wife and four children to take care of, so any move of job would need to take them into consideration."

At that moment two handsome ladies swept into the room; hair coiffed high on their heads and wearing elegant long gowns. Hal turned, relieved to be let off the hook from his 'interview'.

Momentarily he was unable to see which was the younger. They could have been sisters.

"Willie my love, I have missed you." The one who had entered second crossed the room quickly and embraced Willie giving him a kiss on the cheek before taking his arm and turning in one fluid movement to face Hal.

"Hal, I have heard a lot about you from Willie. This is an unexpected pleasure to meet you. Let me introduce my mother. Mother, this is Hal Slater, Willie's good friend who has come to join us for dinner. I can see that you have already met my father. Has he been grilling you?"

"Now then, my dear, that's a trifle harsh; would I ever do such a thing! Anyway you are embarrassing our guest."

"Yes, Father. You always do when you meet clever young gentlemen." She turned quickly again to Hal.

"I am sorry, Hal, we did not mean to make you feel unwelcome in our house. Now come over here and sit beside me and tell me all about your wife and family."

Hal could see who was the dominant person in this household. Willie had certainly let himself in for an interesting life. As they talked he came to like Kate's direct manner; she was quite happy to concede a point when proved wrong in the lively discussion over the dinner table. Hal's discomfort with his ill-fitting suit was soon forgotten as he was drawn into the family conversation.

The evening soon drew to a close with carriages being called. While William made his goodbyes from Katherine, Charles Deere drew Hal to one side and speaking softly, came straight to the point.

"Hal, I like what I see of you. Should you wish to join us at Deere's at some time, we could use your agricultural and business knowledge on our management team. Just get in touch should you consider it and we will come to some arrangement. Don't leave it too long as we have a lot happening at present with advances in agriculture. We aim to stay in front with new machinery."

Hal considered the offer over the next few days. He really liked the idea of getting back to his roots in farming. It had all come as bit of a surprise to him, but by the time he returned home to the usual loving welcome from Maggie and the children his mind was made up, bar one thing. He needed the approval of Maggie. That evening once they were alone, he approached the point carefully.

"I had dinner with Willie Butterworth and his fiancée at her parents' house when I was in Moline; very pleasant people, you would like Katherine."

"Oh yes. When do they get married?"

"Charles Deere offered me a job."

"Oh yes. Did you accept it?"

"I did not say yes or no. I wanted to hear what you thought about it. It would mean moving to Moline."

She put down the embroidery she was working on.

"Hal for Heaven's sake. Why don't you just tell me what you think. You know we will go wherever you want. I know you well enough that you have already decided that it is a change you want to make. When will we go?"

"Well, I haven't said anything to Mr Deere yet. I wanted to make quite sure you would not mind. I suppose it would not affect the children too much, and Doris could come with us to continue looking after them. There will be good schooling there I am sure; I can ask Willie. I will send word to Mr Deere and then go across to see him and can look for accommodation."

"No, you get the job and then I will find a house. If I am having to move then it has got to be just right."

Hal travelled to Moline. He was appointed as part of the management with particular responsibility for the development of steam tractors.

As the world started into the new millennium the Slater family moved to Moline. Hal became deeply engrossed in his work with Deere's. He could not have been happier than when he escaped his office and was able to get his 'hands dirty', tinkering with engines and talking to farming folk. Three years later he became interested in the use of the gasoline engine to provide power in the field, particularly in the 'tractor' developed by John Froelich of the Waterloo Engine Company of Iowa. It took him another fifteen years to persuade the Deere directors to buy up this Company and to compete with Henry Ford's mass-produced Fordson tractor.

THE BIRTH OF FLIGHT 1905

18

The family soon settled into life in their new home in Moline. Hal became so engrossed in his job at Deere's that Maggie complained on more than one occasion that she hardly ever caught a glimpse of him. A year after their move, Sean, aged sixteen, joined Deere's as an apprentice, followed a year later by his younger brother Jason. Hal was insistent that they should learn the trade starting at the bottom.

Peter was the extrovert of the four. When his time came to leave schooling he had no idea what he wanted to do, except that he did not wish to follow his father and brothers in their chosen careers.

Eventually Hal and Maggie decided that they would have to direct Peter's thoughts for him.

"Peter, come to my study. We must have a talk about your future, you can't go on hanging around here doing nothing."

Hal had worked hard from an early age, overseen by his father, Stephen. He had been brought up on the farm that work started at day break and finished at dusk on six days of the week and on the seventh day you went to church, morning and evening. Not that he was any longer a regular churchgoer and only expected his family to attend when he did.

"Come in, lad. Sit down. Now what about continuing your studies by going to Yale?"

Hal, although not a rich man, was by now quite able to fund a place at one of the smart places of further education.

"Father, I don't think I could spend more time studying. I know I am going against yours and mother's wishes, but I am just not a 'book' sort of guy. Sean and 'Jas' are enjoying their training, but I want to be free and able to follow whatever comes my way and make my own life."

"Well, that is just not acceptable." Hal was beginning to lose his patience with Peter. "Everybody has to have a job or be in training. How would you support yourself without an allowance from me?"

"I don't want to be rude, Sir. You and mother are always telling us how you came to New York with just the clothes you were wearing. You both made a success of your lives, starting from nothing. Why can't I do the same?"

This rather took the wind out of Hal's sails. He could not but admire the young lad's spirit in standing up to him and sticking to his principles, whatever they might be. Though for the life of him he could not see what they were.

"Hmm…Well you are right there my boy. Your mother and I did have a degree of luck though, I have to admit. I tell you what: I will continue your allowance for another six months, after that you are on your own. I hope you will have found something worthwhile to be doing in that time."

"Thank you, Father. One day you will be proud of me."

"Oh, don't think for a moment that your mother and I are not proud of you now. Your brothers and sister too" he added kindly.

Later as Hal and Maureen sat after dinner, Hal with a night-cap of whisky in his hand, he commented gruffly:

"You know, my dear, that boy of yours" (they were always 'her children' unless they had achieved something special, and then they were 'his') "is very like what I must have been at his age. Ambitious. Confident in himself. Keen to make his way in the world. Headstrong. Speaks his mind. And handsome of course," he said with a broad smile.

"Do you know something, 'old man'? You have a very high opinion of yourself and a very swollen head! But you are probably right about one thing. I expect you were handsome at Peter's age and now you are just a gnarled old man, but in spite of that I still love you." She came over and kissed the top of his head. "I am away to bed, you may join me if you are not too 'sozzled' from your whisky" she said, from the doorway, turning and giving him a coy teasing smile. She could still rouse him when she was in a flirtatious mood. She really had not changed from the young girl he had met so many years ago on the ship.

Two days later Peter was ready to leave. He had found an old carpet bag of his father's in the attic, stuffed a spare shirt, trousers and boots in it, emptied his savings into his pocket, and went to look for his mother and father.

"You going so soon, Son? I thought you would hang around for a few days to get your thoughts together."

"No, Father. I only have six months less two days in which to make my fortune!" He said this without malice and a big infectious grin on his face.

| EIGHTEEN

"Oh, I see" Hal blustered, rather taken aback by Peter's audacity, but they had always had a good father/son relationship. "You know I did not really mean what I said. You can always count on your Mother and me if you run into difficulties." He could not help but think back to his brother George in those far off days in Devon. He remembered how distressed his father had been that he had not been closer to him when the lad got in trouble.

Maggie came flouncing in, her long skirts held up at the front in both hands.

"What's this then? My little boy leaving his doting mother?"

She was trying hard to put a brave face on this parting and not to burst into tears before he left.

"Come now, you can't go with just one shirt, and I will have Doris put you up a lunch box."

Peter had not been totally honest with his concerned parents. He had been thinking a lot about his future, ever since he had read about two brothers who had the December before achieved their ambition to create a flying machine. Wilbur and Orville Wright had managed powered flight in their Kittihawk air machine at Dayton, Ohio. Not a long way, but it had excited Peter enormously as he avidly read everything he could glean about the Wright brothers. He was determined that he wanted to make this his career. The thought of soaring effortlessly up into the sky and clouds like a bird had him dreaming like a love sick beau. When his thoughts did return to earth he realised that his parents would never hear of him risking his neck in such a mad scheme. Just because two mad brothers had supposedly got their feet off the ground did not mean that Peter could fly like a bird.

He was determined that he would go and try to get employment from them. He would at least learn all about their theories of flight.

As he started on his long journey across Illinois, Indiana and into Ohio, it never occurred to him that perhaps the Wright brothers would not need an 'apprentice', or that there might be others with the same aspirations as he had. Uppermost in his mind were the two thoughts... his excitement of flight, and that his father had started with nothing.

He arrived at the train station in Dayton, tired, feeling dirty, homesick and not as enthusiastic as he had at the start of his journey. What the hell! Here he was, he might just as well go and ask. At the very least he might get a glimpse of the flying machine.

Outside was a man unloading crates from the back of one of Mr Ford's new model motor vehicles.

"Please, Sir. Can you direct me to Mr Wright?"

"Well, young man. You would be meaning, I expect, either Mr Wilbur or Mr Orville. You somehow look as if you would like to fly, but you will have to grow better wings than you have at present. Don't read about Icarus though. You might get a nasty bump." He started chuckling at his own joke.

Peter continued to stand in front of him, certainly not amused.

"Do you not believe, Sir, that they can fly? The Mr Wrights, I mean. Mr Ford has made a car that you obviously find useful. My bet is that a few years ago you would never have thought that you would be using a gasoline-driven carriage. It's the same with flying. A few years from now flying will have been developed. It is the next great step forward that man is going to make. Don't mock a great invention, Sir."

"Well, well. What do we have here then? A proper little fire-brand. If you feel that strongly about it you had best be getting along. Down Main Street, second block on the left, you will see Wright's bicycle shop. Flap, flap along then, sonny." He broke into guffaws of laughter this time as he turned to heave another crate out of the car.

"Thank you, Sir," Peter replied stony-faced. How could anybody be so stuck in their ways and inward-looking and so downright stupid, he thought to himself as he picked up his carpet bag and turned to set off down the street.

"Hey, young man. I am going that way. Would you care for a lift, you look fair tuckered out. I was only pulling your leg, you know. Everybody round here is mighty proud of the Wright boys."

Peter half turned back. "No thanks, I would rather walk." He was still feeling cross inside, even if it had been a bit of harmless fun.

He stopped on the way for a doughnut and a drink. Deep in his own thoughts he chewed his way through the stodgy greasy bun. He knew he was right. Flying and mastery of the air was going to be the way forward. What the Wright brothers had achieved was just the first step in the development of the aeroplane. One day travelling by air would be for the adventurous and not just for the Wright brothers. Peter planned that he would be one of the adventurous, he was going to fly. This was just the beginning of that dream.

19

The bell over the door of the bicycle shop tinkled as Peter pushed his way in.

Pushed his way in was an understatement. From floor to ceiling the space seemed to be covered in wheels, bicycle frames, tyres and every other conceivable part of a bicycle one could imagine. Across this jumble was a low counter, with a youth leaning on it, forearms either side of a comic book, his shoulders and tousled head shaking as he laughed at the pictures. He looked up as Peter stood in front of him. A smile still on his face as he stood up erect. He was probably only a couple of years younger than Peter.

"Can I help you, Sir? A new bicycle? Or a part you require?"

"No, none of those, thank you. I wish to speak to one of the Mr Wrights, please."

"Well, I don't think that is possible at this time. I am here on my own. Mr Orville is away at the 'factory' and Mr Wilbur went out two hours ago and I don't know when he will be back, or even if he will be back today."

"In that case I will just have to wait, won't I? I will go out and sit on the step. When you see him, please tell him Mr Slater wishes to speak to him."

He was tired after his long journey and the disappointment of not meeting the brothers. It had never occurred to him that they might not be there. Soon the warm sun lulled Peter into dozing as he leaned against the wall.

He was awoken by a tread on the step. He looked up dazed with sleep, his vision blurred as well by the sun shining in his eyes.

"You found your way here then I see, young man."

He rose to his feet.

Peter realised that this was the same man he had met at the station. He really did not want to get into another discussion over the merits of flying with such a bigot.

"Yes, Sir. I am just waiting to see one of the Mr Wrights." He slumped down again to lean against the wall.

The shop door opened and the tousled-haired youth stuck his head through the gap.

"There was a Mr Slater here to see you, Mr Wilbur, he said he..." He looked down and saw Peter leaning against the wall.

Peter was scrambling to get to his feet again when the gentleman put his hand on his shoulder to restrain him.

"Thank you, John. As you can see, we have already met." He lowered himself gingerly down to sit next to Peter. "The last flight I came down a bit heavily and jarred my back," he explained. "I gathered you wished to see me, Mr Slater. Wilbur Wright at your service!"

For a moment Peter was flummoxed, he still felt half asleep. "My apologies, Sir, for what I said at the station. It is that I have a great belief in flight and I had no idea who you were."

"Apology accepted. Maybe it is I that should apologise to you as I was making fun of you. Now let's start again. What can I do for you, though I think I can guess."

"I was hoping that you would be able to give me a job. I am a hard worker and don't mind what I do and only need enough to live on. I just want to learn all about flying and aeroplanes..."

"Hold it, hold it a moment. I know all about your enthusiasm. You are Mr Slater, I know that much. Do you have a given name? What training do you have? Where are you from? You sound educated. What of your family? Do they know you are here? A lot I need to know about you."

"Yes, Sir. I am Peter Slater from Moline, Illinois. My father is head engineer of the tractor division for Deere's. I have had a good schooling. My father would have liked me to either go on to college or start an apprenticeship with Deere's, but I wanted to make my own way. My father does not know I have come here, but he gave me six months to prove myself. I just want to find out all about flying and ..."

"Stop, stop, give me a chance to catch up!" Peter had been rushing on hardly drawing breath. "What exactly do you think you could do to help my brother and me? We are only just developing our ideas, which in many ways are quite different to those of other inventors such as Lilienthal and Pilcher with gliders and we of course have built and added a gasoline engine. Now I am getting carried away with my enthusiasm!"

"I am quite happy to do anything, Sir. I have always been quite good at drawing and model-making if that is any help. Please, Sir, I just want to learn about flight."

"Right, Peter. We will give you a job on trial for a month and see how you go."

| NINETEEN

"Oh thank you, Sir. Can I start today? Where should I go?"

"No, you may start tomorrow morning. Be here at seven. First though you need a good night's sleep. Go another block down here and take the fourth avenue on your right. Two hundred yards down on the left you will see a white picket fence, nice house and garden in front of it. Ask for Mrs Barterelli, she is a widow and I am sure will give you a room. Say I sent you. Off you go then, be here at seven sharp."

Peter's tiredness had left him; he almost danced down the street in his excitement at having been given a job with his heroes, the Wright brothers. Fleetingly he realised that no mention had been made of any money, but what the hell! He had his allowance from his father to keep him going for six months.

He easily found the white picket fence. The neatly kept garden had brightly coloured hollyhocks growing against the two storey clap board house which had a shingle roof. He rapped the brass knocker on the door.

An exceptionally attractive, tall, slim lady opened the door, her hair piled neatly on the top of her head, long dark coloured dress tightly buttoned at her neck. Peter judged her to be in her early forties. He had been expecting someone much older, not that he had really thought about it, but in a passing thought had assumed a widow would be old. She smiled sweetly at him.

"Hello, what can I do for you?"

"Mr Wright thought you might have a room to spare. He has just given me a job," he said excitedly.

"Well that's good news. He is a very kind man, is Mr Wilbur. I assume it was Mr Wilbur you have met as I know Mr Orville is away in Carolina again. Well then, let me see. I do have a room in the attic that you could have. Come in and let's go and have a look. You look tired. Have you been travelling far?"

"Yes Ma'am, I have come from Moline, Illinois. It was a long journey, but I wanted to get here as quickly as possible."

"First let me give you something to drink." She led him into a kitchen, the range glowing snugly on the far wall; floral-patterned curtains enclosing the mullioned windows. It reminded him of home and he felt momentarily homesick.

"A glass of hot milk suit you, and perhaps a cookie?"

"Oh yes please, ma'm." He realised how hungry he was, the doughnut he had had earlier did not seem to have even filled a corner. The homelike kitchen reminded him of the large meals prepared by his mother to satisfy his brothers and himself.

"Now then, let me get a few things clear in my mind. Firstly, you must have a name!? Secondly, I appreciate your politeness in calling me, Ma'am; but I would rather be called Mrs Barterelli, please."

"Yes ma'... Sorry Mrs Barterelli. I am Peter Slater."

"Next Peter, a few house rules, which my two daughters and I try and adhere to. No smoking or spitting in the house, though I am sure you have neither of those bad habits. We take it in turns to lay and clear the table. You will bring your laundry down on Monday mornings and leave it by the boiler. I would like to know if you intend to be out for the evening meal or out late. I will put together a bite to eat and a can of tea for your midday break. That will do for now, so let me show you the attic room." They climbed the polished wooden staircase. All the furniture and ornaments glowed with a sheen that could only have come from careful care; not a spot of dust to be seen anywhere.

"That is my room and that my daughters'. This is the bathroom. You may have a bath weekly, we will arrange which day. The attic is up here." She led the way on up a narrow stair, but still well polished.

"There, how does that look to you? Will you be comfortable and happy in here, do you think?"

"Oh yes, Mrs Barterelli. It looks more than adequate. I expect to be working most of the time. I want to learn as much as I can about flying."

"I hope Mr Wilbur will not work you too hard. You must have time for some relaxation. My daughters and I often have a singsong round the piano on a Sunday evening. I hope you will join us. It would be nice to have a bass or tenor to add some harmony. You do sing, Peter?"

"Well not really, but I am prepared to have a go."

"I will leave you alone now. Come down when you are ready. We eat at six. How does a dollar a week sound? Let me know when you come down." She was off out of the room before Peter had time to think.

He unpacked his few belongings and then lay on the bed to consider his situation. 'Everything had gone pretty well really. He had been offered a job by the Wrights; found very comfortable lodgings. I wonder what the daughters will be like? Probably just as annoying as my little sister Maureen!' With that thought he drifted off to sleep...

"Peter, Peter. The tea's on the table. Come on down."

He leapt off the bed, pulled on his boots, and bounded down the stairs. Feeling cross with himself and thoroughly embarrassed that his very first meeting with the family he should be late.

"Come in and sit down here." She indicated a chair opposite the two girls sitting demurely waiting to start. He could feel himself blushing a bright red. The younger of the two sniggered quietly into her hand.

"That's enough of that, Patience." Mrs Barterelli scolded. "Peter, let me introduce Ethel and Patience. I should think, Peter, that you and Ethel are much the same age. She is just risen sixteen, Patience is thirteen."

| NINETEEN

"Mother, I am sixteen and several months. Anyway you should not disclose a lady's age," she said rather primly.

"Oh, who is blushing now? Anyway you are not a lady yet," teased Patience.

"You are just an annoying little sister, just a worm." Ethel replied.

"That's quite enough of that. What will Peter think of you two?"

"Actually I am quite used to it, Mrs Barterelli. I have a younger sister. So that we all know about each other, I am seventeen."

Conversation became much more relaxed and general. The family all wanted to hear about his family and where he lived. By the end of the meal Peter was feeling completely at home.

20

Peter was outside the bicycle shop before seven the next morning. Wilbur arrived in his Ford; pulling up in a cloud of pungent exhaust fumes.

"You will be working down at the factory, Peter. That's about a mile out of town. Can you ride a bicycle? If you cannot you will just have to learn quickly! Come on round the back and let's find you one." He was off without waiting for a reply. The shop's back yard looked like a bigger version of the inside of the shop. Wilbur seemed to know his way around in the jungle of parts. He delved in and came up with a serviceable-looking bicycle. Peter was relieved to see that it was not one of the 'Ordinary' bicycles, or as they were called 'Penny Farthings', which had been so popular up to a few years ago. This was a rather tired looking 'Safety' bicycle which had the now standard equal sized wheels.

"Load it up in the back of the truck and we will go on down to the 'factory'."

The 'factory', when they came to a juddering halt after a rough, bumpy ride out of town, consisted of two large wooden sheds.

"Now then, Peter, how much do you know about the principles of flight?"

"Well Sir, really nothing at all. Only what I was able to read in a paper about your historic flight last December. It did say that it was only possible because the air moving over the wings created lift, whatever that means, which meant that the machine rose from the ground."

"That is a very basic idea, but it is a start at least. The wings are the important bit, as you have read, but the shape of the wing, by which I mean its curved cross-section; the size in proportion to the weight it is to lift; the position of attachment to the body; the control surfaces on the wing or elsewhere on the machine. All these affect the stability in the air, that is assuming that they have got the machine into the air! Come on inside and I can show you what I mean."

"You mean to say that you actually have a machine here Sir?" Peter just could not restrain himself with excitement. He was going to be face to face with a real aeroplane. Maybe even to touch it or possibly sit in it. This was more than he had dreamed of.

"Peter, this is where we are developing our machine. Of course we have one here. What did you expect?"

They went in through a small door on one side. The shed was poorly lit, but sufficiently for Peter to be able to make out the strange looking machine sitting on two trestles with another at the end of each wing. It looked very much like the blurred photograph Peter had seen in the paper. He did not quite know what he had been expecting, but he had a sense of disappointment. The machine was just a muddle of bits of wood held together with wires and the wings covered in white cloth. Surely this thing could not have flown. It had no engine or apparent means of moving. Wilbur glanced sideways at him and saw Peter's sceptical look.

"She does not look much, does she? I can see by the look on your face that you think I am having you on again! Of course she does not have the engine and propellers in her at present. Come here and let me explain more about what I was telling you outside. Let me start from the beginning. This wooden framework holds it all together and the wires, which are tensioned, gives the whole structure strength. The engine fits on here and drives, by chain, two propellers which are mounted on these brackets. As you can see the wings and control surfaces are covered with stretched cloth. One of the important things about flight is the reduction of drag. You understand what I mean by that? No, I thought you didn't.

"Drag is the resistance an object creates by moving through the air; when we drive along in the motor vehicle or ride a bicycle the air flows past us like a wind. The bigger we are the greater the wind feels. That is the resistance. The more there is the harder it is to push the object along. The harder it is the more power we need. More power means a bigger engine. A bigger engine means more weight. More weight means we need more lift.

"That brings me to the wings. To create lift the wings need to be slightly convex on the bottom which means that air moving past the wing has to go faster over the top than underneath, this produces lift. Of course to produce lift the air has to be moving over the wing and we achieve this in two ways. Firstly, the engine and propellers are pulling the machine through the air, so like when you ride a bicycle the air is moving past. Secondly, if we are flying into the wind it is blowing past us and over the wings. Are you keeping up with me so far?"

"Yes I think so. If I fixed wings on my bicycle and pedalled as hard as I could, then I might fly?"

"Well yes, in theory. However, there is rather more to it than that. I have not mentioned about weight. The lift produced by the wings of a certain size with air moving over them at a certain speed will only give so much lift. So the weight of the machine with its engine, pilot and gasoline have to be kept to a minimum. Henson back in 1842 built a flying machine driven by a 25 hp steam engine. It never got off the ground. It was too heavy. So you see there is a very fine balance to be maintained."

"It does all sound rather complicated, Sir. To be honest mathematics was not my strong point at school. It seems to me that you must be able to do a lot of calculations to design a flying machine."

"Oh, you need not worry about that, young man. All you will be doing to start with is making the tea and sweeping up the floor!" Wilbur said with a twinkle in his eye.

"Right, come in here and meet Mr Taylor. Charlie is our chief engineer. You will be working for him. Listen to him and you will learn. He is a very knowledgeable mechanic and an expert with engine construction and flying machine design."

They went on through the back of the shed into a lean-to extension, brightly lit by the morning sun flooding in through the windows running down the whole of one side. Bent over a wooden bench, running the length of the windows, was the back of a tall, brown-overalled man; cap turned backwards with the peak only partially covering his shoulder-length hair.

"Charlie, this is Peter Slater who I mentioned to you yesterday. He is coming to work with us for a month to see how he gets on."

"Hello Peter. Get your coat off, you will find an overall on the hook by the door." This was said without a break in the work he was engrossed in, as he continued to bend over the bench, without turning.

"I never mentioned anything about payment." Wilbur stopped as he went to leave the workshop. "I will pay for your lodgings with Mrs Barterelli for the next month. How about that? Then if you are staying on we will have another talk about it."

"That will suit me very well. Thank you Sir." Peter got his coat off as instructed and joined Mr Taylor at the bench.

"Now this is the engine from 'Flyer 1', and the propellers." He indicated the two wooden double bladed propellers lying further along the bench. Peter guessed that 'Flyer 1' must be the machine flown at Kitty Hawk last year and the one sitting on the trestles next door.

"We plan to use the same engine later in the year, hopefully, in 'Flyer 2'. I am stripping the engine right down and will rebuild it so it's as good as new."

At last he straightened his back and smiled at Peter. His eyes were a bright blue and his large bushy moustache reminded Peter of pictures he had seen of a walrus.

| TWENTY

"Here, grab that wooden stick with the rubber on the end and you can start grinding in the valves. Put a little of this grinding paste round the seat of the valve and push the rubber suction cup onto the top of the valve and start twisting the stick between the palms of your hands, like this… Keep going until there are no signs of any pitting in the valve seat. Then you can move on to the next one. As you can see, this is a straight four engine, of 12 horsepower. Water-cooled."

Peter set to with a will, but it seemed to be a very slow job and soon his arms and hands were aching with the continual twisting. However time flew by as he listened, enthralled by Mr Taylor's continuous talk about engines and how he and the brothers had developed and constructed the flying machine from what they had learnt from their work on gliders.

The light began to fade. "That will do for today, Peter, you have done well. Tomorrow we will be able to start reassembling."

21

Every day was a new adventure for Peter. Sometimes he worked with The Wright brothers on the new construction of 'Flyer 2'. This was what he enjoyed the most. Working with the white pine, to construct the frame and struts. The brothers were hoping that this would give the same strength as the spruce they had used before but be slightly lighter. They were also reducing the curvature of the wing, to try and minimise the effect of drag.

One day towards the end of his trial month, Peter had been thinking, as he worked at painting the wings of 'Flyer 2'. "Mr Taylor, I cannot see how this machine is going to get into the air. All it has is these skid things underneath. I can see that they would allow it to land at the end of the flight, but the drag would be too much for it to become airborne. I know that drag is so important."

"Yes, you are quite right. We have not seen much of the brothers since you started here. The reason is that they are busy out at Huffman Prairie, outside of town, constructing the launching ramp and catapult to get this fine machine into the air."

"Oh, I see. The catapult will give it that first bit of air flow over these wings. I suppose it will be pointing into the wind as well, and that will provide enough lift to get it into the air."

He got on with the painting as he thought more about the machine and flight. His imagination began to run away with itself as he pictured in his mind that it was him lying flat on the wing as the machine was shot into the air.

"Come on boy, pay attention to what you are doing. You look as if you are in a dream." Mr Taylor admonished.

"Sorry Sir. Yes I suppose I was. I was thinking about the controls once it was into the air. The ailerons on the back of the wings are used to give extra lift for taking off, but I am not clear what the other controls do."

"Yes, they are, but they are also used for turning. If you raise or lower the aileron on one side it creates more drag and the machine swings that way and

| TWENTY-ONE

goes up or down. Basically you have three different controls. No, sorry it's four. Ailerons, I have explained. Rudders at the back, also for turning and stabilizing the machine to keep it on a straight course. The elevator at the front, which balances the rate of climb or descent with the power of the engine. The one I forgot is of course the engine. There you have it. Easy, isn't it! Of course the clever part of being a pilot is to balance all four controls together."

"Would you like to fly Sir?"

"Oh no, not me. Definitely not. No, I would not want to do that. I am quite happy doing what I do. My missus would never hear of me going flying. Oh no, definitely not."

"Now young Peter you have been with us for a month. I have spoken to Charlie and he seems more than pleased with what you have been doing. As you know we are coming up to a busy time with the trial flight of 'Flyer 2', and need the extra help. So if you want we are prepared to keep you on. I will continue to pay Mrs Barterelli for your lodgings and give you five dollars a week. I have said nothing to her so you will make sure she is prepared to put up with you. I expect you enjoy the company of that pretty young Ethel anyway!"

Peter's face reddened. He had to admit to himself that he was attracted to her. He had noticed how she was often flirting with him.

"Thank you, Sir. I am really looking forward to seeing the machine fly."

"Well don't get too excited. Things don't always go to plan."

'Flyer 2' was ready to go by the middle of September, except that the wind continued to blow too strongly in the wrong direction for the take off. Then, on the twentieth, dawn broke with a gentle breeze in the right direction. All was made ready and Mr Orville climbed aboard to lie flat on his stomach just to the side of the engine; clad in leather jacket and helmet, goggles over his eyes, boots firmly placed on the rudder controls; the engine was started with a cloud of white smoke blowing back over the pilot until it was deemed sufficiently warmed up by Charlie Taylor. Peter felt very proud to have been allowed to do the job of holding one wing up to balance the machine while it rested on the prepared glideway. Mr Wilbur was on the other side, shouting instructions to Mr Orville, which he could either not hear over the engine noise or was ignoring. Wilbur had explained to Peter that he had to run as hard as he could to support the machine until he could feel it begin to rise or he could not keep up, but on no account was he to pull back or down on the wing. Take off was a critical time for a flying machine. At this time it was at its most unstable until it had made sufficient speed. Any tug on one wing would be enough to tip it into the ground.

Peter could just hear Wilbur's shout of… THREE, TWO, ONE, GO… He felt the wing leap forward under his hand and started to run as never before.

Then it was gone, as he tripped over his own feet to tumble head over heels on the ground. He looked up to stare in wonder as the machine rose away from him into the air, the wings wobbling slightly up and down as Orville juggled with the controls. Soon it turned to fly round in a circle to come over Peter's head as he still lay on the ground filled with wonder and amazement.

"You alright?" Wilbur shouted at him. "On your feet; we never know where or when it will come down. You must be ready to get out of the way."

Orville continued to circle left and right for several minutes and then again heading into the breeze prepared to come back to earth as gently as possible. Peter could see that this was a critical moment again. The skids only had to catch on a lump of grass or earth and the whole thing, at best, would end up on its nose sitting on the elevator; or at worst flip sideways or onto its back. Orville stopped the engine moments before the skids touched and worked the elevator control to try and lift the front of the machine as it met the ground. The skids made contact quite heavily but did their job for several yards before the machine halted and gently leaned forward onto the elevator. Peter ran with the others to support the wing once again as it finally came to rest.

The brothers were jubilant at another successful flight safely achieved without any great damage to either machine or pilot. They immediately went into deep discussion leaving the machine in the loving care of Mr Taylor and Peter.

"Oh my. That was quite something. It was truly amazing. I never thought I would ever see anything quite like that."

That evening as he bicycled back to his lodgings he was still full of the excitement of his day. He could not wait to tell someone about it all. Mrs Barterelli and Patience, disappointingly, seemed to be not very interested, but Ethel could not take her eyes off him and seemed as excited as he described every moment of the flight and the preparations beforehand.

He was not a great letter-writer and his correspondence home was fairly infrequent, usually at Mrs Barterelli's insistence, but on this occasion he needed no prompting to tell them the exciting news.

As he cycled in to work the next morning, his mind was still focused on the landing in particular. It seemed such a dangerous and casual way to finish a great achievement. He was staring down at the ground in front of the bicycle wheel, not paying any attention to where he was going; after all he did this early morning ride every day and very rarely met anybody or anything. Suddenly, right in front of the wheel, a jack rabbit dived out of the field. Peter just had time to swerve to stop hitting it, hitting instead the low grass verge on the edge of the road. The front wheel bounced over this obstruction, catapulting Peter into the air, but he was still firmly gripping the handlebars before he returned uncomfortably to the saddle, and sliding off into a heap of legs, arms, and bicycle.

He sat there, winded for a moment, but thinking of what had happened. He had not gone over the handle bars, the wheel had ridden over the obstruction (even if it had been uncomfortable), no serious damage had been done to him or the machine. Why could they not fit bicycle wheels to the flying machine? He collected himself from the tangle, leapt on again and pedalled furiously down the road before his great invention and contribution to the development of flying machines should be lost.

"Mr Wilbur, Sir. I've had a great idea."

"Now what would that be, Peter?"

"Well, Sir, why can we not fit some bicycle wheels onto 'The Flyer' instead of the skids? I am sure that it would make it safer for landing and would stop the machine tipping onto its nose." His mind was still racing away in his excitement. "I believe it could help with the launching as well. Maybe we could do away with the catapult and ramp too," he rushed on. "If we did away with those then we would not be confined to waiting for the wind to be in just the right direction."

"Hold it a minute, whoa… You will have designed a whole new machine before the morning is out," Wilber said with an amused smile on his face. "Actually Orville and I have been considering this idea. It is only sensible. I am very pleased that you have been thinking about it as well." He put his arm round Peter's shoulders when Peter's face had fallen on the news that it was not his unique idea. "There is one slight problem though. Which is only a matter of development, nothing that we cannot get over… That is weight… We have got to get more power from the engine and more lift from the wings. The wheels will then be a necessity. Now, as you have become such a great designer." he said not unkindly. "I want you to start making some scale models that we can test in the wind tunnel we are building to study the flow of air over and round the machine."

"Oh yes, I would like that, Sir."

22

Development with the Wrights continued over the next few years with flights getting longer and longer and with more turns and manœuvres. Peter was becoming keener to advance his theory of flying from the ground to actually getting into the air, as the pilot. He realised that this was not going to be possible while he was at the Wrights. They had been of enormous help to him in giving him a job in the first place, but it was now time to move on to something else. It was at this time that the US Army Signals Corps began to show an interest in developing an airborne capability, realising that the extra height gave an increased view of a battle front and better reception for the poor wireless communication.

Peter joined the army, not quite knowing how it would get him into the air. Hal and Maggie were horrified that his aspirations should be going down this track. It was bad enough that he was joining the army, let alone a branch that would pose such danger as flying. However, they had never been able to have a say in the course of Peter's life, so they did not press it too hard now.

Peter was welcomed by the Signals with his knowledge of the Wright aircraft. Especially so when they purchased the Wright Military Flyer. He was transferred to College Park, Maryland, where this aircraft was based. He was given his first chance to pilot from here. The aircraft was not much more sophisticated now from the 'Flyers' that he had known and still had not acquired any wheels, which was a disappointment to Peter.

With his heart in his mouth he took his position on the aircraft, feet firmly planted on the controls and he was off on his first flight. He immediately lost all his fear as he soared into the air. His exhilaration unbounded. He turned at the end of the airfield and came back gaining height for his turn again before coming in to land into the wind. The skid touched as he pulled back to raise the nose which he had seen the Wrights do so often. He was down safely without any damage.

Military flying went ahead by leaps and bounds over the next few years, with war in Europe looming ever larger; in 1913 the Signals Corps bought from

TWENTY-TWO

Britain several A.V.Roe 504 Ks, a proper biplane with wheels and a large front-mounted engine This was what Peter and his colleagues were training on and teaching others to fly. The way flight, in war time, was to be made the best use of was by attacking ground positions by the dropping of grenades, or by rifle or machine gun fire from the side of the plane.

While the dreadful slaughter went on in the trenches in France, aircraft development and more sophisticated ways of delivering destruction both to the ground and in the air were thought up. These filtered through to the USAF.

Whenever Peter had the chance of a few days' leave he would often return to Dayton to stay with Mrs Barterelli, and in particular to see Ethel. Each time he would worry that she might have found herself a suitor and would be courting. He was not yet feeling he was ready to take a wife and indeed had not met anyone whom he was so attracted to as Ethel, but she was not going to wait for him forever.

In the spring of 1917, after once again arriving unannounced with the Barterellis, and having volunteered to join the American Eagles, an American Squadron of pilots fighting with the allies in France, he decided that he would ask for Ethel's hand to be engaged and married on his return from France.

Neither Mrs Barterelli nor Ethel were taken with this idea as the young couple were by now aged in their late 20's, and there was the uncertainty of war too. However there seemed to be no choice as Peter was already assigned to the 8th Aero Squadron and could leave for Europe at a few days' notice. They were flying de Havilland DH-4s, a dual seat plane which was used for bombing and observation duties.

The squadron reached England eventually early in 1918 and were very frustrated to have to undergo a period of training prior to leaving for Le Havre and the front. Their duties were mainly on the observation of the front line as it waxed and waned through the summer of that year and into the autumn when, mercifully, the Armistice was signed and Peter was able to return to his patient fiancée in Dayton.

The marriage was a quiet affair for the thirty-year-old couple. The Wrights were there of course and Peter's parents, brothers, and sister came down from Moline.

Ethel was soon pregnant. They had wasted no time in starting their family; however Peter was out of work having left the Army Air Force on his return from France. His one passion still was flying, so he was determined that his career should be continued in the air.

So when Duggie Smit, his great pal from his army days, approached him and suggested that they set up together in business as a Barnstorming team,

Peter jumped at the idea. It did not go down too well with Ethel though. It would mean he was constantly away from home, and with her impending confinement was not at all popular. She had been living with her mother, Mrs Barterelli, since their marriage and Peter eventually conceded that this would continue while he did six months of barnstorming with Duggie, but he would return for the birth of the baby.

The first thing was for the business to acquire two Curtis JN-4 aircraft from the army. They had both, like most pilots, trained and done their active duty on this plane, the Jenny. Because the Jenny had been produced in very large numbers it was now being sold off at a fraction of its production price. The team scraped together the $400 needed for the two aircraft, which left them very little in hand to get them started to buy fuel and any spare parts they might need.

The idea of barnstorming was to fly to a remote small town, overfly it doing a few manœuvres to attract attention before landing in the field of a nearby farm to negotiate the use of the field as a temporary airfield, then another run over the town to drop leaflets advertising the air-show for the next day.

Duggie and Peter had decided that they would start the show with some spectacular loops, rolls and turns. All done at as low a level as possible with very low level runs over the assembled crowd to make them duck. Next they put on a mock aerial combat show, finalising with one of them going out of sight behind trees or a barn and dropping a large smoke bomb to simulate the plane crashing. They would both land back in unison and offer ten minute flights for the public. These were very popular, even at the price they had to charge, particularly with the young ladies who thought that these men were real heroes.

Six months of this was enough for Peter. The money to be made from it was very variable; sometimes it would not even cover their costs. They spent the time going from one out of the way town to another, living out of a suitcase, often having to sleep under their planes. There also seemed to be an increasing number of 'circuses' doing the same sort of thing and having to think up increasingly dangerous stunts.

Not the way for a newly married man to be living. He returned home after five months but was immediately bored by his enforced inactivity and living with three bossy women. He did retain his Curtis so was able to get away from time to time and lose himself amongst the peace of the clouds.

Ethel's time arrived and she went into labour attended by her mother and the midwife. The birth was a complication from the start. The baby was a breach coming feet first. After a day Ethel was worn out and the contractions grew less and less as she became weaker and weaker. Peter did not know what

| TWENTY-TWO

he could do to help, each time he appeared at the bedroom door he was sent away. It was not the place for the father to be at this time. He paced up and down and could not settle at anything. In the early hours of the morning at last he heard the new-born cries of the baby, at last he was allowed into the room and was able to hold his son, who in spite of the great struggle to enter the world was a strong and healthy baby. Ethel was totally exhausted, sleeping and not looking at all well.

Over the next few days she showed no interest in the baby, or in recovering, lying in bed sleeping most of the time and not eating. Peter and his mother-in-law became more and more worried as her temperature rose and she became lethargic and eventually dropped into a coma from which she did not recover. Eight days after the birth Ethel died in the bed where the baby had been conceived and born.

Peter was absolutely shattered, blaming himself though not knowing what could have been done differently. He lost interest in his new son, not really wanting anything to do with him. This made life in the Barterelli house even more strained than it would have been anyway.

It was at this time of his deep depression that he met up again with Duggie Smit, his barnstorming partner. They applied for and got a mail delivering contract from the Postal Service. This involved delivering letters round the country from town to town. It inevitably involved Peter being away from home for extended periods of time. The baby, now called Brad, was brought up by Mrs Barterelli and Patience, Ethel's sister.

Peter, when he did get home showed only a passing interest in Brad. As the years rolled by he remembered the boy's birthday but that was really all.

In 1925 the Airmail Act was passed through government which brought in all sorts of controls on licensing of pilots and aircraft, aids to navigation and eventually to an early form of air traffic control. With these new safety regulations came the wish of the travelling public for travel between cities for passengers. Peter and Duggie, as just a small business, lost their mail contract. Unable to expand sufficiently to keep up with the new big Airline businesses, they decided that if you could not beat them it was better to join them. Both applied for and were accepted by the new United Airlines, flying Henry Ford's new passenger plane, the Trimotor 5, carrying up to 13 passengers in the all metal, very noisy plane

Peter's working life continued with this company as it grew and grew, and he became one of its senior pilots. As for Brad, he saw his father from time to time. He inherited his love of flying and doted on his grandmother and aunt, who guided him through his formative years of high school and college.

BACK TO ENGLAND 1942

23

Brad arrived by train at the dockside in New York with his small group of fellow officers. Although he had known from his embarkation orders that he would be travelling from the U.S. by ship to England, it was a surprise when he was directed to board the R.M.S. *Queen Mary*.

He remembered clearly the excited reporting in the press of the maiden voyage of this great ship in May 1936. The British certainly knew their stuff when it came to building great luxury Trans Atlantic liners. He also thought back to the accounts he had read as a boy of the disaster of the *Titanic*.

"I hope we don't sail so far north into 'iceberg alley'; though at this time of year we would have to take a very northerly route to suffer the same fate," he thought. "On the other hand there are other hazards in the time of war, like the U-Boats, but why worry, there is nothing I can do about it. It's best to just lie back and enjoy the trip."

As he looked up from humping his kit bag onto his back he was amazed at the size of the ship in front of him. The great slab of her side rose above him with the wing of the bridge sticking out at the side, and behind that the three enormous funnels, smoke gently curling out of the front one in the light breeze. The fact that the whole ship was painted in a matt grey paint from waterline to the top of her mast came as rather a disappointment to Brad. He thought it demeaned the 'lady' to be seen in her working clothes rather than her pre-war finery of black sides, startlingly white upperworks and bright red funnels with black tops: The colours of the Cunard line under whose flag she sailed.

He clattered up the gangway, following the rest of the company travelling with him, entering through the side. Once again he felt awed by the vastness

| TWENTY-THREE

and could imagine the splendour of earlier years, though now where possible she had been converted, he later discovered initially in Australia, to accommodate up to 15,000 service men on every trip across the 'pond'.

He checked in at the 'reception' desk and was allocated a cabin on 'D' deck. This he was to share with 3 other lieutenants who were unknown to him. 'D' deck was easy to find as all he had to do was climb up the grand staircase leading straight out of the entrance hallway until reaching the clearly marked level. That was the easy part.

Finding his allocated cabin in the rabbit warren of passageways and cross passages was another thing. They were very narrow, to allow as many cabins as possible to be fitted into the available space. Every time he met another person, equally well loaded with luggage, they had to squeeze past each other passing the kit bags over head.

The cabin, when at last he located it, seemed to be just as small. He reckoned that the four of them would have to have a rota for getting in and out of the bunks. These were one above the other on each side of the narrow alley up the middle; a small desk with cupboard under was at the opposite end to the door with two shelves over it. The bunks could not be more than two foot six wide with headroom to just allow the occupant to sit up without bending his neck. Hopefully, this was not going to be too long a voyage.

Two of the bunks already had kit bags thrown down on them. Brad chose the bottom bunk of the ones left, thinking that it would be less hot and stuffy than being close up under the ceiling. A small printed instruction leaflet was on the desktop. Brad picked it up to give it a quick glance, but then having seen how it started thought he had better read it more thoroughly.

SAFETY INSTRUCTIONS.
TO BE READ BY ALL OCCUPANTS

Lifebelts are to be carried by all men while the ship is at sea. (They are stowed in the cupboard under the desk.)
On hearing three long blasts, repeated at minute intervals, on the ship's siren. All men should muster at their abandon ship position.
Officers should check their muster lists.
Await further instructions from the ships officers or person in charge.
Do not carry anything with you other than warm/waterproof clothing.

YOUR MUSTER STATION IS THE FORWARD PART OF
THE 'F' DECK MESS HALL.

As Brad finished reading, the door opened and a kit bag came in closely followed by a short, dumpy, dark-haired man, with a small cigar hanging from the bottom of his lower lip. He looked to be about Brad's age.

"Fucking hell! What a way to go to war! Hi! Mike Warren," he drawled as he extended his hand over the top of his kitbag; at the same time rolling the cigar from side to side.

"Hi! I'm Brad Slater, pleased to meet you. I guess we are going to be sharing this chicken coup. I'm from Illinois and you sound as if you come from Texas," Brad replied, as he was pushed back against the desk by the kit bag advancing further into the cabin.

"Now how did you guess that, I wonder?" Mike's face broke into a wide grin; A grin that Brad was to discover very rarely left his face whatever the circumstances.

"Don't tell me, you must therefore either be a cowboy or an oil driller!"

"Man, you must be psychic! Pretty close guess on one count, actually I was training to be a geologist. What about you?"

"Well, I came straight out of college and started the training to be a teacher. But as I have English blood in my veins, I thought I had better help the old country out for a while. I joined up when they looked as if they could do with some help when the war with Germany did not look as if it was going so well. I was all set to move to England..."

"Heh, you must be mental or something to actually volunteer for this sort of thing," Mike interrupted.

"Yes, probably; anyway the Japs put paid to that idea last December when they sneaked up on Pearl Harbour. I decided that the good old US of A needed my help straight away, and I got drafted just like you I imagine."

Mike seemed like a live wire, full of energy and obviously enjoying the excitement of what was ahead of them.

"Come on, I am going to do a little exploring of this old tub." He struggled to push his kit bag up onto the top bunk.

"Here let me give you a hand. What the hell have you got in there? It weighs a ton!"

"Not much. Just a few goodies to take over for the poor starving Brits! I thought I might do a bit of trading for some Scottish whiskey! Being a short ass sort of guy rather reduces my reach!" he said with an infectious laugh as he and Brad put the kit bag on the bunk. Mike turned out of the cabin door and was off down the passage like a rabbit down a hole.

Brad had soon lost him in the jostling crowd, but thought he would for a start try and find his muster station at the 'F' deck mess hall, apart from which he might get a cup of coffee there.

| TWENTY-THREE

He assumed correctly that 'F' deck would be two below his cabin level. It would seem, in an emergency situation, rather strange to be going downwards. One would think that safety lay in the open air by going upwards. 'His was not to reason why… etc.' he thought; others with more knowledge than himself had planned it.

Although with the short experience he had of Army planning it did not fill him with confidence, he was also correct in his assumption about the coffee; in fact it was the smell of coffee that guided him there. This then was where he would have to find his way to in a hurry. He realised that he was not carrying his life belt, in harbour there was probably no necessity, but it would be easy to forget when leaving the crowded cabin.

Ascending 'blindly' up Brad came out on the open deck. He had a good view from this height over the quayside, which was a hive of activity as hundreds of servicemen climbed aboard up the two gangplanks. The bridge wing rose above him for, he guessed, another three decks. By leaning outwards against the solid wood rail he could just make out forwards the shape of the bows and by peering up, the outline of the rows of lifeboats. Looking backwards he could see the curve of the ship disappearing towards the stern. This was certainly quite an experience and for a short while Brad forgot about the war and the possible perils ahead.

Further down the deck he saw Mike leaning on the rail, still with the cigar stub in the corner of his mouth. Brad strolled over to him.

"Quite a sight. Isn't it?" he said, meaning the ship, which he had been thinking about.

"Oh sure. All the best of American manhood struggling off to war. With no idea of what they may be in for in a few months' time," he said rather cynically. He seemed to have lost much of his bounce and enthusiasm of earlier. "Well Brad, me boy, what is your part in this great adventure? Tell me how you came to be here and what you are expected to be doing." His grin reappeared like the sun coming out from behind a cloud.

"I mentioned that I had volunteered. Quite simple really. I have my pilot's licence which I got at college and thought that I would be able to fly fighters or bombers. Not a bit of it, they said my eyesight was not good enough. I was then drafted into the 101st Airborne, 327th Glider Infantry as a glider pilot. Hence my shoulder flash of pilot's wings with G in the middle. The G stands for Guts!"

"You're kidding me. It must stand for Glider. What bad luck though to sign up and then not get what you wanted. How come you got a civil licence with bad eyesight but are not good enough to fly ops? Come to that you are OK to fly gliders."

"Oh that's simple. Flying a glider you are only going downhill all the way and only for a short distance and often it is best not to be able to see too well! What about you. What's your outfit?"

"Nothing smart about me like being a pilot or anything. I am just an ordinary G.I. Not even a volunteer, just drafted!"

That evening, of late Thursday September 1942, Brad and the thousands with him left their homeland mostly for the first time ever, to travel to a foreign country to fight a war. Where it would lead them, what part they would play, even if they would ever return home, only the future would tell.

24

Life onboard ship soon established a boring routine. The two meals a day, which had to be organised in several sittings, broke the monotony of the card schools and reading. Brad spent a lot of time on the open deck enjoying the surging, effortless progress of the great ship through the Atlantic waves. It was only after the ship had sailed that they had been told that their destination was Scotland, a little town called Gourock where they would anchor and be boated off.

During one of Brad's afternoon 'musings' on deck; he was joined by a young 'Limey' ship's officer.

"Hello soldier. Enjoying your luxury crossing?" he enquired leaning on the rail beside Brad.

"Thanks for asking, but No! It's pretty boring. I will be glad when we reach this place Gourock."

"Oh, you won't be staying long there. You will be moved on to some training camp."

"You are one of the ship's officers by the looks of you. Tell me about your job and about this ship. That's if you have the time."

"Yes of course. I have five minutes before I go on watch. I'm Jim by the way. I am a very lowly person, one of the 4th officers; at everybody's beck and call it seems sometimes! I am just about to go up on the bridge to keep the first dog watch with the 2nd officer."

"Now steady up a bit. What's a dog watch for heavens sake? I'm Brad Slater from Illinois by the way, pleased to meet with you."

"Alright, let me educate you with nautical language. You landlubbers are dead ignorant about the sea and ships," he said with a twinkle in his eye.

"OK, OK, I know you sailors all reckon you are the cat's whiskers! I would still like to know about dogwatches while we are on the subject of pets. Don't tell me it's how they tell the time either. I really am a landlubber. This is the first time in my life I have ever been on the sea."

"I'm sorry I did not mean to be rude. I realise living in the middle of such a vast country it stands to reason. Anyway about these dogs. The day is divided up into six watches of four hours each; except the watch from 1600 to 2000 hours, which in your language is 4 p.m. to 8 p.m., which is divided into two dogwatches of two hours each. This was so the crew had time to relax after the day's work and both watches would have time to get something to eat. However, at sea when on duty we treat it as an ordinary four hour watch."

"Ok, I've got that but why is it called a dog watch?"

"I am not really sure, but I think it comes from way back. There are several theories about its origin, but probably it's a derivation from 'Dodging a watch' as it's only two hours. Look I must be off now. I will be 'keelhauled' if I am late for my duty. See you around." Jim went forward towards a ladder.

"Thanks Jim. Next time we meet I want to know about being keelhauled and more about the ship."

Jim turned at the bottom of the ladder.

"Good to meet you Brad. Let's meet here tomorrow, same sort of time." He hurried off.

Nice friendly sort of chap, Brad thought. For a Limey, he added to himself.

The next day as planned they met up again. Brad discovered that Jim came from near Plymouth in Devon. He was the youngest of three, with two elder sisters who were both serving with the Women's Army Corps. His parents farmed, but Jim had always wanted to join the Merchant Navy and to see the world. He realised that it was a disappointment to his father that he had not stayed on the farm. Perhaps one day he might leave the sea and return. Anyway he felt he was being more useful to the war effort in this job.

"Now yesterday you left saying you did not wish to be 'keelhauled'." More of your nautical language I suppose?"

"Yes, just trying to intrigue you! It was a punishment back in the days of sail. A rope would be passed right under the ship from side to side, the ends tied to the arms and legs of the offender. He was then thrown over the side and dragged from one side to the other. He would nearly drown depending on how long it took to pull him through and he would be badly scraped on the barnacles on the ship's bottom. Not very pleasant. Thankfully it's been given up, but the expression is used to denote getting into trouble."

"Tell me something about this great ship. I would love to have sailed in her before the war. It must have been the height of luxury."

"I agree, nothing could have been spared. Although not everyone travelled first class. The steerage class was the cheapest. I have only been in the ship for about a year so never experienced the luxury travel. As I think I mentioned yesterday, I am a very junior officer having been in training before. Enough

| TWENTY-FOUR

about myself. You wanted to know about the ship. Coincidentally, she was launched almost exactly eight years before we sailed on this trip – actually the day before, on 26th September 1934. She sailed on her Maiden Voyage eighteen months later. She is one of the biggest ships ever built at over 81,000 tons. Is 1020 feet long. The steam turbine engines develop 116,000 Horse power to enable us to do 32 knots maximum speed, that's about 40 miles per hour."

"Phew, that's quite something. She must take quite a bit of stopping with all that weight and speed. I must say it's a very easy ride in spite of the waves. We get to Scotland tomorrow, is that right?"

"Yes, I think we should anchor early evening if all goes well. This is of course the most dangerous part of the voyage, so it is possible we could be delayed and then would probably get there the next morning."

"Why is it more dangerous now than yesterday, for instance? I would have thought we were travelling so fast we are pretty safe and we are changing direction all the time."

"You are right in a way. The zig-zag, which is why we alter course regularly is to make it more difficult for the U-boats to get a fix on us. However we are now within range of German aircraft. Just think what damage and casualties a couple of bombs would do. Ships are all too easily sunk by being bombed. We British have had plenty of experience of that all over the world in the last three years. On the previous trips I have done we have been joined by a Royal Navy Anti-Aircraft Cruiser and several destroyers to make sure the Germans can't get near us. We should sight them tomorrow morning after breakfast if all goes as before. That's a job I would not like to be doing, as you will see in these sea conditions. It really makes me feel sea sick just to look at them. Well, time flies. I must be off to earn my crust! See you around before we get there, Brad. Cheerio chin chin."

They were a funny lot, these Limeys. However if they were all like Jim they could not be bad sorts. They seemed to run this ship pretty efficiently, and from all accounts they had put up a good fight against the Germans. They sure could do with a bit of a help out, by all accounts, at this time. Anyway, that is what he was here for.

True to Jim's word, when Brad went on deck the next morning, three small ships soon caught his attention; he could just make them out on the horizon ahead of them. He watched them for a while as they gradually drew closer. It would appear that while the *Queen* was maintaining her zig-zag course the little ships were ploughing on keeping straight ahead, as they did not seem to change direction.

After about an hour the two smallest ships did change course and veered off to the right. As Brad watched them pass by at about a mile distant, though he found it difficult to judge distance accurately, he recalled Jim's comment yesterday about seasickness.

These two ships were behaving more like corks on the water than ships. Each time they met a wave the bow buried itself and white water flew upwards and outwards before they bobbed to the surface again and then plunged head first down into the trough before starting the cycle all over again. They were never still for a moment; conditions must be intolerable, wet, cold and exhausting. What a way to fight a war, Brad thought. He was glad he had volunteered for the Army, or rather really the Air Corps. At least he would have his feet on dry land, except of course when he was airborne, but that he loved. He went below for the midday meal and met up with Mike who as usual was one of the first to get his feet in the trough.

"You scoffing again Mike? I can't for the life of me think where you put all that grub. You never take any exercise. You would not be so keen to fill your face if you were on one of the little escort ships I have been watching." Brad went on to describe the way the little ships were being tossed about.

"Oh, they are used to it; I need to get stoked up while I can," he drawled. "It's their war, I did not choose to come. I am going to make the most of it while I can. Anyway, I've got a good poker game going and I am on a winning streak."

Brad felt disheartened by Mike's attitude. It was their war as well. Just think what the 'Japs' had done at Pearl Harbour and they were allies of the Germans. He decided to return to deck, he might run into Jim again who would cheer him up from Mike's negative thoughts.

He was pleased to see Jim approaching down the deck.

"I thought I might find you here," Jim greeted him as he leant on the rail next to Brad. "If we are lucky you should get your first glimpse of Europe pretty soon. The weather and visibility are quite good. You will be able to see the smudge of the land on the horizon over to the Southeast. That's it over there." He pointed ahead right over the bows.

"Say that is great! Will that be Scotland? Or have you miscalculated and taken us to France?"

"Enough of that, suggesting the navigator doesn't know his job properly. Although if it was me doing the navigating you could have been right," he beamed. "Actually it's the north coast of Ireland."

"Is that so. Now my grandmother came from somewhere in the south of Ireland. My geography never was too special. Now, before I went down to luncheon two of the escort ships seemed to disappear off to the right. Would they be going off to Ireland? You were certainly right about them having a rough time."

| TWENTY-FOUR

"Yes, they were detached to their base at Londonderry as the sea conditions meant they were unable to keep up with us, so could be no help if we needed it. You saw how they were 'shipping it green' over the bows and right back to the bridge. Oh, I suppose I should not have told you where their base is, though everybody must know. Come to think of it there can't be many spies out here!"

"Now hold on a minute, you are leaving this old landlubber behind again. What is 'shipping it', was it 'green'? I won't tell anyone where they came from!"

"Shipping it green, is when the bows of the boat go under a wave and the sea floods over the deck. Anyway they would have difficulty in shooting down enemy aircraft bobbing about like that. I bet they would have a jolly good try though. My goodness, we are getting very close to the old cruiser over there. She is not far ahead of us now… Oh that's good, we are starting our turn now. We will be clear of her. Brad, I have enjoyed our chats; I will be pretty busy from now on and may not have a chance to see you again before you leave the ship. I have jotted down my home address on this postcard if you ever have some leave and would like to meet my family. I know they would be happy to have you to stay for a few days; Of course I don't know whether I would be there."

"Say, that's real kind of you. I don't know where I will be drafted to, as I won't get my orders 'till I am ashore. Should I be near Plymouth, Devon, then I sure will visit with them." He said, as he glanced at the card Jim had given him. "Thank you Jim, it's been a pleasure meeting with you and you have helped to make a boring journey more interesting."

25

They shook hands and Jim left to get on with his duties. Brad resumed his contemplation of the sea and watched as once again the *Queen* turned at the end of her zig, or was it a zag she had just completed, Brad wondered.

The cruiser disappeared from his view as the great ship drove effortlessly through the waves, cutting through them almost head on as she bore down on this leg of the zig-zag. Brad's thoughts turned to his unknown posting once they arrived in Scotland. Later he could not recall why or what made him turn his head to look forward once again.

There, seemingly poised on the front of the *Queen* was the distinct shape of the bows of a pinky-grey coloured ship. A split second later he could make out a twin-barrelled gun turret with guns pointing skywards, sea streaming over the deck and surging back to crash into the base of the turret before flying as a cloud of spray up towards the superstructure of the bridge which now seemed to appear as if in slow motion from round the *Queen's* bow.

Brad gasped and stood transfixed, eyes glued to the scene unfolding so rapidly in front of him, yet each millisecond seeming like an eternity. His first fleeting thought was that this was one of the little destroyers he thought had left them for their base, but almost at the same moment he realised it could not possibly be as it was at least half an hour since Jim and he had watched them depart. Neither ship appeared to be aware of the other or alter course. His brain had time to wonder how they could possibly miss one another, but perhaps the distances were deceptive. This was certainly a closer situation than Jim had commented on earlier. He hoped that Jim was not in charge on the bridge. He could see two sailors standing below the bridge of the ship, immobile like statues, gazing towards the *Queen Mary* with a look of horror on their faces as the great ship bore down on them.

Then suddenly everything changed into double fast time.

The cruiser's bridge came fully into view followed by her two funnels, deckhouses and a stubby mast. Leaning out as far as possible Brad watched as the

| TWENTY-FIVE

'Queen's bows sliced into the side of the cruiser at a 45-degree angle. He felt a slight tremor through his feet and stomach where he was leaning on the rail. Simultaneously a cloud of dust and steam rose from the point of contact. Moments later there was the sound of the collision; a surprisingly muted bang and louder squeal of tortured metal, and the shriek of escaping steam like a boiling kettle.

Then it was all over. The front two thirds of the cruiser slid past below him, lying pushed over on its side; the foremast sticking out away from him, the red weed-covered bottom looking so out of place and small as he looked down on it. No sign of any human existence on what had become so quickly another bit of the war's flotsam.

The wreckage disappeared astern out of Brad's view, he guessed to sink quite rapidly. He remained standing at the rail, his knuckles white from clutching it so hard. His mind trying to analyse the enormity of the scene that had unfolded so quickly before his eyes. It had all been so quick that he began to wonder whether he had imagined the whole thing, as the *Queen* did not seem to be slowing down. How could she have sliced straight through the cruiser without sustaining considerable damage to herself?

Eventually she did slow, but did not stop and ten minutes later she was working up speed once again. Brad felt he had to share his experience with someone even if only to dispel the shock of what he had witnessed. Also he would like to know more about how the accident had happened and news of the cruiser and survivors. He determined to track down Jim before he landed to get the inside information.

He stopped one of the crew to ask if he would get a message to Jim. He realised then that he had no idea of Jim's surname. However, when he said he was a 4th officer that seemed to be sufficient.

"Oh, you mean young Jim Pearson. He stands watches with the 2nd officer. I can't make a promise that I can get word to him, but I will try. Who should I say asked and what did you want of him? He may be rather busy for now, what with what has just happened and our arriving at Gourock."

"Just say that Brad would like to have a word with him if he has the time, meet him on deck. Thanks."

Later, as the sun fell towards the sea through light clouds in a blaze of colours with land now clearly visible on each side of them, Jim appeared at Brad's side.

"Hi. As usual I only have a minute or two. I got your message by the way. What can I do for you? Though I think I can guess. You want to know what happened this afternoon."

"You're right there, buddy! I saw it all, you know, from right here. I hope you were not in charge in any way."

"No, thank goodness. If I had been, it would have been the end of my career as an officer. Officially I should not be talking to you about it at all; it never happened! It will probably just be hushed up, a casualty of this dreadful war. Off the record and don't tell anyone. I am sure I can trust you. Why the collision happened I have no idea. An enquiry will have to sort out who was to blame. Port does give way to starboard according to the rules of the sea. On the other hand the ship being overtaken has the right of way and we were on a zig-zag, as you know. I know that I am glad I am not the Captain or officer of the watch of either ship."

"Have we sustained a lot of damage? We did not stop or slow down for long. Surely we should have been looking for survivors from the cruiser?"

"We are making a bit of water apparently but the full extent of damage won't be assessed until divers can go down. As regards survivors, I can't imagine there could have been many."

"We should have stopped to look, though."

"That is what I thought at the time, but when you think about it we have thousands of you Yanks on board. If we stop to look for survivors we are putting at risk all those lives for the sake of just a few. This is another dreadful decision of war where lives have to be sacrificed to save others. Do you want me to mention that you saw it all take place, or do you want to keep quiet? I am sure there were several others who witnessed it, not to mention those on the bridge."

"Really, I would like to forget about it, but I think you should tell somebody."

"OK, I will tell the 2nd officer and he can pass it on if he thinks it important. Remember what I said about not talking about it. Mum's the word," he said with that infectious smile.

Brad heard no more of the dreadful incident as they continued slowly now up the channel with land on each side disappearing into the fast approaching gloaming of night. The only visible light was the occasional red or green light on the buoys marking the route the great ship had to follow to her anchorage. Every now and then there was the brief glimpse of a shaded light from on shore. This was so different from their departure from New York a few days ago, where at night-time the city was a blaze of lights.

Soon the ship slowed and the rumble of the anchor being released echoed over her. Loudspeakers blared out giving instructions for assembly for leaving the ship. This was Scotland, Europe. Their war was about to start. Brad could not help a sense of excitement but at the same time concern at what the future might bring for him and the thousands of his fellow Americans. He had no doubt in his mind that some of them would not be returning to their

| TWENTY-FIVE

homeland.

Brad did not disembark until the next morning. It took many hours of organisation to unload the GIs, arrange for their units' transportation to the many different camps around the country. During this waiting period Brad was able to catch a few minutes with Jim Pearson. Time enough to renew their shipboard friendship and for Jim again to give Brad an open invitation to visit his family in Devon.

26

At last it was time for Brad to leave the *Queen*, down the gangway to a paddle steamer moored alongside. This old boat had plied its trade for several decades as a ferry, or for pleasure trips around the sheltered waters of the Clyde. On this trip she discharged her noisy, excited cargo of men at Greenock, on the south shore.

Brad received his orders from the office of the harassed quartermasters. A rail pass to a town called Cambridge, from there he was to get himself to the US Army air base at Mildenhall. He was assured that there would be transport from the railway station. The orders seemed to be incredibly vague; no indication of which train he should be catching, to where, how long it might take, when he was expected, or even whether he would be expected at all. Brad felt he could easily just disappear and no one would be any the wiser. This however was war; he was just one of thousands to be kept track of by the drafting offices. He was an officer and was expected to have some initiative! At least there was transport from this dock to the railhead. He slung his kit bag over his shoulder and went out to find one of the two tonners parked outside in the yard. He scrambled up into the back with a mixed collection of men from all three services. The tailgate was slammed shut and they were off at a furious pace. The driver seemed only to have two speeds; Sudden stop, and foot hard down. After five minutes of being tossed around, falling over their luggage and thrown from end to end, the man nearest the cab beat on the roof to get the driver's attention.

"Heh buddy, slow down. You have a human load here. If you go on like this we will need hospitalisation rather than the rail station."

A voice came back over the roar of the engine and the grinding of gears:

"It's OK, man. We are nearly there. I just thought you white trash needed toughening up a bit before you go getting your heads shot off." This was followed by peels of hysterical laughter as the driver creased himself up at his own joke.

| TWENTY-SIX

"Son of a bitch, you black bit of no good. I'll tan your black ass for you when this heap of shit stops."

Anything else was abruptly cut off as they came to a final screeching stop and were all flung in a heap towards the front.

"Let me off to get at that black bastard."

"Slow down soldier. It's not worth starting another war over," Brad replied sensibly, putting a hand on his shoulder to restrain him, as they tumbled gratefully out of the back. The driver knew when he was ahead and remained out of sight in his cab with now just the odd rumble of a chuckle.

It seemed that Brad was the only one posted to this place, Mildenhall. He presented his rail pass at the ticket office which was being overseen by a Military Police sergeant. The ticket clerk looked at the pass, scratched his head, 'hummed and ha'd' for a minute, licked his index finger, and slowly thumbed through a rail timetable.

"Come on, Jock. The war will be over before you have made up your bloody mind. I did not come over here to stand in a fucking queue in a draughty station," the GI behind Brad shouted out.

"Why are you in such a hurry to get to war, buddy. I've come over to try out the British broads," another further down the line added. This raised a laugh and several more venal comments.

"There's no need for that, men. We will get you there soon enough, wherever you are going," the sergeant shouted. "You will 'love it' once you are there and wish you were back in bonny Scotland."

Brad's attention was drawn back to the clerk as he slowly looked up. "Now you see we canna get you to Cambridge without you having to go to London first, laddie. I am not sure that this pass of yours will allow me to give you a ticket for London because it says Cambridge, you understand." The clerk was quite unphased by the ribald comments from further down the queue. He looked as if he had experienced many years of similar abuse.

Brad could not believe what he was hearing. It was no wonder the Brits needed help with this war if this was the speed at which they worked. He looked up at the sergeant for support.

All he got was a shrug of the shoulders.

"Now look here, my man. I am on a very secret special assignment especially for Mr Churchill, and must get to Cambridge as soon as possible. If it means going via London or even Paris, so be it. I can get you in an awful lot of trouble if you will not give me a ticket, but if you do give me one you will really be helping the war effort, do you see? Now be a good chap," Brad said in his best impersonation of an English gentleman, not that he had ever heard one other than on a film at the cinema back home.

"Och well, if Mr Churchill says it's alright then I can do it. I canna give you a ticket for Paris, though. Our trains dinna go there." This was said without a trace of a smile. Brad was left wondering whether it was a joke or the clerk was really so dull.

Along with hundreds of GIs, Brad boarded the train to take him on the first stage of his journey, to Glasgow. Once there he had a long wait for the night train to London. While he waited he was able to get a cup of weak tea and a thick wodge of a sandwich filled with a thin slice of Spam. The tea was almost undrinkable and the sandwich totally indigestible, but welcome all the same, it was served by two friendly elderly ladies half hidden behind a large silver tea urn.

"Do you ladies come here every day?" Brad asked as he chomped his way through the sandwich.

"Oh yes, whenever we are able to get tea and bread. It is not always easy," they chimed almost in unison, "at our age it is not easy to find something useful that will help the war effort. Hopefully this gives a small comfort to you brave boys."

Brad did not feel brave at the present, just rather bored with the long wait. He could feel the sandwich churning round in his stomach. Was this really the sort of food that the British had to put up with? He knew they had rationing over here but that sandwich had been quite something. He wondered what his job would be if he ever managed to get to Mildenhall.

The London train pulled into the platform and there was a rush to find a seat. It was packed with servicemen, civilians, smartly suited bowler-hatted gentlemen, workmen and, it seemed, every other type of the human race. The chatter sounded like Babel; accents from all over the free world: Irish, Scots, English, Canadian, American, French, and what Brad guessed might be Polish or eastern European.

Brad found a seat towards the front of the train, squashed between a lady of indeterminate age wearing a veil covering her face from her firmly fixed hat, and a red faced English soldier in a thick woollen uniform. The whistle blew and, with a lot of puffing from the engine, they drew out of Glasgow station. Soon after a young woman with a small crying baby and a large suitcase looked in the compartment door.

"I don't know whether there would be room for us to squeeze in here? The train is so full and no empty seats," she asked pathetically.

"No, there is certainly no room here," the veiled lady quickly replied, "try the guards-van, or sit in the corridor."

"Here, ma'am, have my seat. I can just as easily sit on my kitbag in the corridor, and you have the baby as well," Brad butted in as he got to his feet. "Here, give me your case and I will put it on the rack."

TWENTY-SIX

During this operation the veiled lady's hat was knocked askew, which caused a lot of muttering. Brad winked at the young woman who gave him a tired smile in return.

"You are so kind. Thank you very much."

Brad moved out to the corridor and stood looking out of the window at the countryside slowly moving past. Evening he realised was fast drawing in as he glanced at his watch. The sun flashed out momentarily from behind a bank of cloud before creeping slowly behind the hills with a spectacular red sunset. Once again he was surprised that there was no sign of any lights showing anywhere. Back home the towns would have been a blaze of neon light. Shortly after, the guard pushed his way down the corridor stopping at each compartment checking that the already dim lights were restrained by the blinds.

Three hours later after being squashed by passing passengers and continual getting up and down from his kitbag Brad was feeling cold, hungry, and thoroughly fed up with the British rail system. The train came to a squeaking halt in the middle of nowhere, or so it seemed, and there it stayed. After half an hour rumour crept down the carriages that there was an air raid on a place called Liverpool and they would not move on until it was over. The young sailor next to Brad nudged him on the arm.

"That must be Liverpool over there, mate. It looks as if they are certainly catching a packet. Cor, that must have been something big to give a flash like that."

Brad turned to the window again. He could see a glow in the sky in the direction and to the right of where the train was headed. The glow was interspersed with regular brighter flashes on the horizon, and the beams of searchlights could be seen where they were shining through what from this distance looked like clouds of smoke.

"What happens at this place, Liverpool, that it is getting such a going over?" he asked the neighbouring sailor.

"A big port and docks, mate. A lot of factories and such like as well. That's where most of the Atlantic convoys end up that come over from your lot. That's to say those of the poor buggers that manage to make it. The subs thin them out something terrible. You are a Yank then? I should not be shooting my mouth off if you are not. One never knows whom one is talking to these days. 'Walls have ears'. No offence meant, of course." He rushed on as if he would run out of breath at any moment. He seemed to have a nervous habit of looking away to the side after every few words.

"Oh yes. I am a Yank, but my grandfather was a Brit. What do you mean 'Walls have ears.' Are you in the Navy then? Is that some nautical term?"

"That I am. Ordinary Seaman Smith, going home for a week's leave with the family in London. My ship has been doing convoy duty up north to the Russkies. 'Walls have ears', no that's just a saying going around meaning that one should be careful of what one says as it might be giving away secrets to the Bosch."

Brad recalled a conversation he had had with Jim on the *Queen* about convoy escort and in particular the Arctic convoys, where the conditions were atrocious. He wondered if Smith's nervousness was a reaction to having been on one of these convoys.

The train just then gave a series of jolts and reluctantly began to move again. Conversations lapsed once again into silence as the clackety clack of the wheels lulled people off to a broken sleep. After another hour they pulled into a dimly lit station. No sign of where they were, but once again the rumour spread, that this was Crewe. A station announcement informed the passengers that the train standing at platform four would be leaving in twenty minutes.

"Come on mate, that's us I think. Let's go find a cup of tea," Ordinary Seaman Smith said to Brad.

The tea-room was bursting at the seams as everybody had the same idea. They pushed their way through the crowd to the serving counter. Brad was surprised to find that the little old Glasgow tea ladies appeared to have doubles serving from behind the big silver tea urn, here, in wherever this place was.

All aboard, the journey continued, until in the early hours of the day they pulled into Euston Station, London.

The tired dishevelled passengers disgorged from the train into the vastness of the station. Some disappeared through various exits while others stood forlornly around as if they did not know where to go. Brad soon spotted two military policemen, keeping a watchful eye on the many service men.

"Heh, soldier. I need to get to a place called Cambridge. Can you tell me which train to take?" After the long uncomfortable night Brad was not feeling in a particularly sociable mood, and was rather taken aback by the policeman's attitude.

"Let me see your travel documents." He held out his hand, staring hard from flinty eyes. This was followed after a pause by "Sir". Brad's pass and ticket were studied carefully, the pass and identification being flicked backwards and forwards and eventually handed back.

"We don't keep a train timetable with us, … Sir. I suggest you try the information office if it is open," he replied sarcastically.

Brad was about to ask if he had some problem with Americans and then thought he had not got the energy at this time of day to get into an argument with the Military Police. He did not like accepting the rudeness, but discretion was the better part of valour.

| TWENTY-SIX

The Information Office was not open, but the refreshment room two doors down had light shining through the steamed up glass. Brad pushed open the door into the fuggy smoke-filled room. This time the tea and sandwiches were being dispensed by a middle aged woman dressed in a flowered 'pinney' with her hair concealed under a neatly tucked-in headscarf.

"What can I get you, ducky? The sandwiches are fresh four days ago, but the tea is only using yesterday's leaves." She smiled and chuckled at Brad's look of horror. "Only kidding you, love." All this said with a broad cockney accent.

"You don't have coffee, I suppose?"

"Cor, love me. What do you think this is then? The Savoy? I have not seen coffee since before this little lot all started. We have rationing over here you know. Not like your lot. That's not to say that we are not grateful for what you send over."

"I will have tea then, please, and a four day old sandwich seeing you recommend them! I have got to get to Cambridge. Would you be able to direct me? The Military Policeman I asked was far from helpful."

"You don't surprise me. Those 'Rossers' are miserable bad tempered bastards. Excuse the language. Now you wanted Cambridge, that would be Liverpool Street I am sure."

"Liverpool Street, you say. I have just last night come past Liverpool. It was having the stuffing knocked out of it by the bombers. You mean I have got to go all the way back up there."

"Na, I means Liverpool Street Station. Here in London town. You wants a number 53 bus from outside o' here, that will take you right there. Just ask the conductor to tell you when to get off. Mind you I don't know if the 53 is running today, what with the raids and that, or you could try the tube."

"I am sorry ma'am, but what is a 53 or the tube?"

"Oh love a duck. I forgot you Yanks speaks another language! 53 is an omnibus and the tube is the underground railway. If you wants to go on that you will see the signs pointing down the stairs just up to the right."

"Thanks ma'am. You have been most helpful."

Brad decided that he would take the bus and he would then see some of the sights of London. He followed the crowd to the exit and out to the steps leading towards the street. So this was the famous London! It did not look much different from any American city really. People were busily rushing about as if they did not have enough time in the day. Come to think of it, perhaps they did not have time; what with the air raids, no street lights to see by as soon as the sun went down, the shortage of food (he had heard that people had to queue at the shops to get bread.), and life must be pretty difficult in general.

151

One difference was the occasional red bus that trundled its way past along the road the other side of the station yard. There were not many cars either. Silly of him, he realised, he had not asked where to get on a 53. The next bus that came along he enquired from the conductress.

"Other side of the road, dear. A hundred yards down you will see the stop. Move right on down the middle to the front," she addressed her passengers. "Hold tight then." She pushed the bell 'Ting ting' and the bus ground into motion and away.

Brad walked on down to a sign indicating a Bus Stop, roughly where he had been directed. After some twenty minutes, as he was beginning to wonder if he would not return to the station and catch the tube, a red bus came in sight. As it got nearer he was able to see that it had 53 displayed on it above the driver's cab.

"Will you take me to Liverpool Street Station?" he enquired from the conductor, a man in his late fifties.

"Yes, I will take you anywhere, that's OK. Hop on then," he replied with a bad imitation of an American accent. "Take a seat."

A few minutes later he appeared at Brad's shoulder leaning casually against the seat across the aisle.

"Where are you from then? I have relations in New York, perhaps you know them?" he asked chattily in a normal cockney voice.

"No, sorry, I am from Chicago, Illinois. New York is a very big place so I doubt I would know them even if I did live there."

"Of course, a silly question! That will be five pence, please."

Brad realised with an awful sinking feeling that he had not got a single coin of English money. It had never crossed his mind. The cups of tea and sandwiches had been free to the servicemen, so he had not at any time since landing needed money.

"Heh buddy. Will you take a nickel? That's all I have got. If you won't I will have to get off and walk." Brad felt thoroughly embarrassed.

"No I can't do that. What is a nickel anyway? I think we can afford to give you a free bus ride this time, considering all the aid you are sending over. Here, have a ticket in case the inspector gets on. I will let you know when we get there, you being new in town." He pulled a five-penny ticket out from his clipboard, smiled and moved on.

They were now travelling slowly down a street with a whole row of houses that were just piles of rubble with the occasional chimney sticking up. The bricks had been pushed back to the side of the road to allow the traffic to get through. As they moved on further east the damage became worse. This must be the result of bombing, Brad realised. Looking up he was startled to see silver barrage balloons hanging in the sky. Through the damage gaps he was just able to make out the cables that tethered them to the ground.

He thought how lucky they were back home. Most people had no idea of the war going on in Europe. It was just sporadic news on the wireless which would be pushed aside by some local trivial event. No bombing and destruction of people's homes and possessions, no food shortages, no fear of invasion and occupation, no loss of loved ones and relatives; though Pearl Harbour had perhaps been a reminder and now here he was and thousands like him, some of whom would not return home. As soon as that started happening the folks would realise. Of course there was the war against the Japs in the Pacific that was just beginning to get going. He had not heard of many casualties from over there as yet, but he supposed they would be inevitable.

Arriving at Liverpool Street he discovered that a train to Cambridge left at midday.

27

Cambridge was reached mid afternoon. Brad was surprised to find an American military policeman standing near the exit.

"Can I help you, Sir? I have transport to Mildenhall if you wish."

"Well now I believe you can. It's almost as if you had been expecting me. This will certainly be the easiest part of my journey."

"I am afraid that is not quite correct, Sir. We have a lot of officers coming through here if they are not attached to any particular unit. We try and meet the London trains, as it is not easy to get to the base from here. I think you are the only one, so if you would follow me we will get going."

The two tonner wound its way through flat uninteresting country for an hour before drawing up at the main gate.

"You need to report to the adjutant's office over there, Sir."

Brad reported to a harassed-looking Captain behind the desk in the office.

"Lieutenant Slater, you say. 101st Airborne?" He ran his finger down a long list of names. "Slater, Slater, no I've got no Slaters here. Well you must be in luck. You can go home now! Just kidding, lieutenant. Go on up to the mess and they will give you a room. I will try and get you sorted out tomorrow. In fact if you report back here in the morning at 0900 I can make use of you until we find out where you are going. Any questions?"

"Not really at the moment, it would be nice to get my hands on some English money. I had a rather awkward moment in London when I needed a bus fare."

"No problem there, Slater. See the paymaster's office tomorrow. See you tomorrow then." He returned to shuffling his bits of paper and looking harassed.

The previous two days of travelling, and the broken sleep of the night before, had left him very ready to drop into bed. A decent meal of a juicy steak in the mess made up for the stodgy sandwiches of the previous 48 hours, and helped to give him a long dreamless sleep.

TWENTY-SEVEN

He met up with the Captain from the adjutant's office over breakfast.

"Morning, Slater. What do they call you? I'm Sean... Sean Wilkinson, from Santa Barbara California."

"Brad. Pleased to meet you Sean, Sir. I come from Chicago."

"Forget about the Sir bit, Brad. Well, if you are ready we will get on over to the office and try to find out what to do with you. Oh, you wanted the paymaster, see him on the way over. Two blocks down and to the right. You will see the sign."

It was easy to find, as Sean had directed. The sergeant looked up from the ledger he was writing in.

"Can I help you Sir?"

"Yes, I need some local money. Dollars don't work very well over here I've discovered."

"That's easily fixed. Did you want to change dollars into English pounds or have them docked off your pay? If the latter I need your name and number."

"I guess I won't be needing dollars for some while. I only have about 20, what will that give me?"

"Twenty dollars will give you £15. That will only buy a round or two of drinks down at the public house or, as we know it, a local bar, in a quaint old thatched house in the village! Give me your name and number as well."

"B. Slater, 4751098. 101st Airborne, 327th Glider Infantry. The adjutant's office had no record of me so I don't know whether you will have better luck."

"That's OK. It's your number that's important. £50 more OK? I don't know when, but it will catch up with you one day."

A really biting cold wind gusted around the huts and low buildings as Brad found his way back to the main gate. He pulled his coat collar up tight round his neck. This was more like the weather back home except that it was a damp sort of cold, not the same as the dry freezing low temperatures he was used to. He thought back to his school days remembering geography lessons about Europe and England. This place was just a small island surrounded by sea, so the cold east wind was coming over water straight from Russia by the feel of it. He shivered inside his thick wool-lined coat. He was glad to get into the over heated adjutant's office.

"Right Brad, I've tracked you down. You should not be here at all! You should have been sent to some place called Swinsbeck in Devon. That's down in the Southwest somewhere. Never heard of it myself."

"Oh that sure is great after all the travelling I've done to get here."

"That's the way it is these days, Brad my lad. There's so many of us coming over here, ready for the big push into Europe, that nobody knows anything. I should think it is a good time to go AWOL if anyone wanted."

"OK, I am not planning on doing that. Now tell me, how do I get to this Swinbury or what ever it is called. More train travel, I suppose. I know roughly where Devon is, 'cos my far distant relations came over from there, but I don't know more than that."

"Let me see. The name is Swinsbeck. It is reached from a place called Exeter, does that mean anything to you.?"

"Yes, I have heard of that. Do you know what I will be doing at Swinsbeck? Is it a camp, airfield, or what?"

"No, this appointment order gives no information at all, other than to say Lieutenant B. Slater 4751098, 101st Airborne, that's you I assume, to report to the commanding Officer, Swinsbeck, Devon, England as soon as possible. Here, I have made out a warrant for your travel to Exeter. You have to go via London. If I were you I would break the journey and take a couple of days' leave there. Go see the sights, have a few drinks, or whatever takes your fancy," Sean said with a large wink.

Brad reversed his journey of the day before to Liverpool Street Station. He thought he might as well take Sean's advice and see what London was like. His bus ride from Euston on his way up to Mildenhall he did not think had really given him the proper flavour of this big famous city that had so much history to it.

28

Sean had told him of the Officers Club near to Victoria, where he would be able to get lodgings. He decided that he should go straight there first to make sure of his accommodation. The club, when he eventually tracked it down, was in an imposing large house that had seen better days; probably as the town house residence of some wealthy family in days gone by.

The large hall inside the front porch was marble floored with a grand staircase rising majestically opposite the front door. Doorways led off in all directions into what Brad guessed were once reception rooms. To the right of the stairs was placed a large desk with a young lady in uniform behind it. She was busy writing and seemed oblivious to the comings and goings of the men in an assortment of uniforms. Dark blue of Navy, light blue of Air force, and brown of Army. Brad noticed that they appeared to be of many nationalities. Americans he recognised easily, others he could see had shoulder flashes denoting their country. As he walked across the hall he saw Norwegians, French, Polish and, judging by the babble of languages, others as well.

The young lady looked up and smiled as Brad stood in front of the desk. He could see that she was in British Army uniform, her service cap struggling to hold her light brown hair in place. Brad judged her to be in her early twenties, from her slim well proportioned figure but difficult to tell from the shapeless uniform jacket and the desk hid her from the waist down.

"Can I help you, Sir?" The smile stayed on her full-featured face which was of an unmade up fresh natural complexion.

"Yes please, Miss. I am in London for a short break in between appointments and need a place to stay. I was told that it might be possible here. Would that be right?"

"That's correct, Sir. I can fix you up with a room if you don't mind sharing. Let me see, you are American. We are quite full at the moment, would you mind going in with Lieutenant Ericson, he is Danish, but speaks excellent English."

"That's OK miss. Beggars can't be choosers!"

"How many nights will that be? I will need your name, identity papers, travel warrant which will I expect show where your appointment is."

"I think I will just stay over for a couple of nights as I should not delay for too long. These are my papers and my warrant." He dug them out of the inside pocket of his jacket.

She took them and started to write the details into the ledger in front of her.

"I see you are being posted to Devon, Mr Slater. It's a lovely county, you will enjoy it I think."

"Oh you know Devon then, Miss. Do you know this place called Swinsbeck?"

"No, I can't say I do. Perhaps I should have heard of it as my home is in Devon, near Plymouth."

"It must be quite a small place, not a big town. Say, I met a guy on the boat coming over who came from near Plymouth. His name was Jim Pearson, an officer on the *Queen*. He was a very nice guy and we got on really well. Wait a minute, he gave me his address and said to call on his folks if I was anywhere near. Maybe you will know the place where he lives."

"Stop right there, Mr Slater. It's a very small world. My name is Jill Pearson and Jim is my little brother. How is he? I have not heard for several weeks."

"Well I'll be darned. Jim's your brother, I can't believe it. As you say it is a very small world. Of all the people I could have met, it had to be you.!"

"That does not sound very complimentary, Mr Slater."

"Oh I am sorry, Miss Pearson. I did not mean it like that. It's just such a surprise, of all … "

"I know exactly what you meant. I was teasing you as you looked so flabbergasted. Anyway, please call me Jill. Any friend of Jim's is a friend of mine."

"Now Jill, this may sound very forward of me, but could I take you out to dinner this evening, or perhaps tomorrow evening. Oh my goodness, there I go again. Jim never told me, maybe you are married or something?"

"Brad, that sounds a splendid idea. This evening is no good as I am on duty here until ten tonight. Tomorrow would be lovely. I tell you what, tomorrow I have the day off, why don't we spend the day together and I will show you the sites of London, if you like. To answer your question, no I am not married or even something. Let's say we will meet here at eleven. Now I really should stop gossiping with you and make it look as if I am being useful round here."

"That is real kind of you, Jill. I would never know what to see or where to go. You can tell me all about your lovely county of Devon too, and I can bring you up to date on young Jim. I will look forward to eleven tomorrow."

| TWENTY-EIGHT

"Cheerio then. Be good this evening!" she said with a twinkle in her eye.

Brad felt he had fallen on his feet. He was going to be shown the town and in the company of a pretty girl too.

He climbed the stairs and found Lieutenant Ericson sound asleep in the twin-bedded room they were to share. Ericson, on waking proved to be a likeable fellow of Brad's age. He persuaded Brad to join him and a group of his friends that evening on a 'tour' of the town. Shortly before midnight Brad felt he could no longer keep up with the party of Scandinavians, who seemed to have hollow legs where drink was concerned, and took himself off back to bed.

Jill was as good as her word the next morning, arriving to collect Brad on the dot of eleven.

"Now, what would you like to see. What are your interests?"

"I really don't know, Jill. I've heard of the River Thames and your parliament, but other than that what is there to see?"

"Buckingham Palace where the king and queen live, Tower Bridge, The Cenotaph, Downing Street where Mr Churchill lives. A lot of the museums and galleries are closed of course. We could go shopping in Oxford Street, not that there is much one can buy, anyway you Americans seem to have most things already."

"Hold it, hold it! That is more than enough for one day. Let's start with the Parliament and Buckingham Palace. After that we can see. How does that sound?"

The hours flew by. They did not get to see all that they should have as they were so busy talking; finding out about each other and there lives up to that point.

As the light failed on an overcast autumn evening, Jill linked her arm through Brad's. He glanced down at her quite surprised at this intimate gesture.

"Say, Jill, my feet are killing me. You've walked me off my feet. What say to round off what has been a perfect day. You lead me to some nice little restaurant where we can have an enjoyable supper."

"I don't know about the peaceful bit, that depends on Hitler. It has been cloudy for the last few nights, so thankfully there have been no raids, though it has not been so bad since this time two years ago when the raids were almost constant; during the Battle of Britain as we call it."

"You know I feel almost guilty that over in the States we are not aware of what this little country of yours has suffered. Bombing, food shortages, no street lights, the threat of invasion, to name just a few of the things that you have had to put up with."

"We are still smiling, though. Talking of food, I know of a little place not too far from here, if your poor Yankee feet can make it, we have no petrol you know! We should be able to get a half decent meal there."

"Lead on!" They linked arms again and set off.

Two hours later as they left the restaurant, Brad jokingly commented,

"That was quite one of the worst meals I have ever had! Tough steak, I hate to think what it really was! Warm watery beer! You called it a half decent meal, what on earth would an indecent meal be like?"

"What do you expect, this is war time. We were lucky to get meat at all. You Yanks are just spoilt! Now I tell you what. You will have to come and spend some leave on my parent's farm in Devon. Then I can show you what real steak is like."

Brad stopped and took her arms, facing her. "Yes Jill, I think I would really like that."

29

Brad caught an early train the next morning from Waterloo to Exeter in the West Country. He had no idea what he would do once he got there, but he seemed to have been lucky so far with the people he had met. His thoughts went back to yesterday and the very pleasant day they had spent together. He had really liked Jill and they had got on so well together. He looked forward to seeing her again, if it was possible, at her parents' place in Devon.

The clikety click of the wheels soon had him dozing off to sleep, only to be awakened by the jerk of the train each time it stopped at a station. He had had just about enough of the English rail system by now. It seemed an age since he had started on his meandering by train across the length and breadth of the British Isles. He would be glad to get to Swinsbeck whatever it turned out to be, so long as it had nothing to do with trains.

Early afternoon found him on the station platform at Exeter. An old porter directed him to a room next to the ticket office marked with the sign 'Service Personnel Enquiries.' This was manned by an elderly sergeant, feet up on the desk, nursing a cup of tea, and a cigarette hanging from the corner of his mouth. For a moment Brad wondered why the whole of England seemed to be staffed by geriatrics. He then realised after a moment's thought, that all the young men and women were either in the services or working in factories helping the war effort.

"Hi there, Sergeant. Busy I see." This comment did not produce any immediate reaction other than for the cup of tea to be slowly put down on the desk and the cigarette to be rolled to the other corner of his mouth.

"What would you be after then, young man?" The cigarette remained glued to the bottom lip, wagging up and down with each word.

"I am Lieutenant Slater, American Army Air Force. I would like transport to some place called Swinsbeck, please."

At last the feet came off the desk. "Now is that so, I thought as much. I've had one or two of you Yanks needing to get up there, not that I know where it is mind, some secret camp is it then? Not that you would tell the likes of me, though. These places seem to be popping up all over the country. We are restricted as to where we can go and all. Now my old dear up in Nottingham is not able to get down here to live, you know. She was only saying…" Brad had had enough of this old duffer's monologue.

"Sergeant, please I need to get to Swinsbeck."

"Oh yes, certainly Sir. If you walk up the hill there you will come to the city centre. You need to catch the auto bus to Honiton." He pulled a large watch and chain out from his uniform top. "If you hurry I believe there may be the evening one leaving in half an hour or so."

"For heaven's sake, man, I have just come through some place called Honiton on the train. Now you tell me I have to go back there by coach. What sort of a place is this country?" The old sergeant looked somewhat affronted at Brad's outburst.

"Sorry buddy. It's just that I have been pushed from place to place with nobody knowing anything."

"Well Sir. It's like this …"

"I should like to stay and have a yarn with you: but there is that bus that I must not miss." Brad was relieved to get away before the old timer got going again.

As he walked up the hill towards the city centre he was appalled to see the bombing devastation, just like it had been in London. Was every city and town in England like this, he wondered?

After asking, he found the little old bus about to depart. Unlike his previous journeys he enjoyed this trundle through the countryside. The route seemed to meander from side to side, he felt, visiting every little village along the way with passengers getting on and off carrying all manner of baskets, parcels and packages. A large middle-aged lady took the seat next to him. After a while he got into conversation with her. She spoke a different dialect of the English that he had heard spoken since he had landed in this country, and he had some difficulty in understanding what she was saying.

"Where'm to, my love? You's one of them Americano soldjers then?"

"I am going to Honiton and then on to a place called Swinsbeck. Do you know it?"

"Do I knows it. 'Cors I does. I'm lived two mile from Swin'beck all my life. Never been further than Exeter in all my time. I knows it alright, you'm going to that there new camp and airydrome I expects."

"I don't know what I am going to! That sounds pretty silly, I expect, not knowing why I am going there. How do I get there? Can you give me directions? How far would it be?"

TWENTY-NINE

"Now dun you'm fret your pretty head about it. You just stays with ol' Bet when we get to Huniton. I will see you or'right!" She gave him a toothless grin and turned to her neighbour across the aisle and was soon deep in unintelligible conversation interspersed with cackles of throaty laughter; Brad could not but help thinking it was at his expense.

Eventually the coach rolled into Honiton. An attractive town at first glance. The main street really wide flanked with houses and shops. Some on a raised pavement above the road, others with the pavement shut off from the road by a two-rail metal fence. This reminded Brad of the hitching rail to tie your horse to in some prairie towns back home. The rail seemed to stop suddenly for no reason, looking as if it had been cut off at ground level. Old Bet noticed him looking at this as they alighted from the coach.

"Them's where we have market of a Saturday. Them's been and take aways most of t'cattle rail."

"Why's that then?" Brad asked, knowing that he was likely to get a long explanation.

"War effort then. To make them there ships and thins. Them's been and collected all the iron and 'aluminum' pots and pans, that to make them Spitfires. Come along then, if you wants to reach 'Swinbeck' before dark. You'm would have a tidy hike if you 'loses' me" she chuckled to herself. "You'm might never be seen again if you'm got lost in the lanes after dark." This time she burst out with her cackly laugh at her own joke.

Brad grabbed his bag and hurried to follow her as she set of at a cracking pace, big basket on the crook of her arm.

"Where are you taking me?" Brad asked as he caught up with her.

"'Swinbeck', of course, my lover. I got to drag my Jack out of the Red Cow first off. He'm will be in there pouring the mild an' bitter down h's throat as if he were never goin' to have another drink."

Brad decided that it was easier not to ask who Jack or the Red Cow were but to just go along with this charade. After all he was in no great hurry to join his unit, whatever it was, another few hours would not make a difference. He wondered for a moment why Jill did not speak like Bet, seeing she came from Devon too. He must make a point of seeing Jill again, and as soon as possible. They had got on really well. Jim had been very friendly too. They must be a nice family.

Bet disappeared from the street while his thoughts had been elsewhere. One moment she was there and the next gone. She could only have disappeared into a doorway. He looked up at the house in front of him. Written on the wall in big red letters it said RED COW. He understood now, this must be a bar or such like. As if by magic Bet appeared again dragging a scrawny little man by the arm.

"Yanki soldjer meet my old man, Jack. He will try and drive us up to Luppit', that if he is not too far gone in drink."

"Now you'm just hol' on Bet my dearess'. You'm will giv' this brave soldjer the wrong idea."

"Oh shut your hole and get round the back for the car."

Jack dutifully did as he was told and a few moments later a small car wheezed its way to a stop in front of them. By now it was becoming quite dark.

"You'm hop in back, and we'm soon'll be there." Brad struggled to fit himself and his kitbag into the back seat while Bet plonked herself in front. Brad feared for the little car with such a big load, and even more so as they ground up a steep hill. He could see nothing outside what with his kitbag blocking the view one way, Bet's bulk in front of him and the fact that Jack seemed to be driving without lights through narrow lanes. Fumes from the exhaust wafted up round him and he had just got to the point of deciding he would rather walk when they came to a juddering halt.

"We'm there. You'm jus' come inside for a bite to eat 'fore Jack takes you'm on to 'Swinbeck'. Leave that there bag in car."

They were in front of a thatched cottage, standing on its own in a lane with high hedge banks all around. As far as Brad was concerned they could be anywhere.

Bet pushed open the wooden half door and a waft of warm wood smoke-smelling air came out to greet them, followed by a large tabby cat miaowing a welcome as it rubbed itself against Bet's ankles.

"Come in then. Don't stan' around, Jack, carry basket in. Sit at table, soldjer. Tabitha get from under my feet." The instructions were issued in a machine-gun-like burst The last salvo being directed at the cat as Bet busied herself at the black range, glowing redly through the bars at the front of the fire box. Bet stabbed logs of wood into the already red hot fire. Within minutes the kettle on the top was boiling merrily away and puffing a gout of steam as if it was fit to burst.

The delicious smell of newly baked bread wafted across as a loaf was produced as if by magic from a crock, smartly joined by a pot of homemade jam and a pat of bright yellow butter. Brad suddenly realised that he was extremely hungry.

"What them call you then?" Bet asked as she poured tea into a large mug.

"Brad, Brad Slater, Ma'am. I'm from Illinois."

"Now I wudn't knows about any place called Illinoise. That wud be in Americer I suppose. A little village or a town the likes of Huniton or even a city the likes of Exeter?"

"No, Ma'am. Illinois is a state in the north near to Canada. I suppose you

TWENTY-NINE

could liken it to this place Devon."

The conversation gradually established a more exact description of Brad's home, though he realised that Bet and Jack really had no conception of the size of the United States. The tea and thick slices of bread with raspberry jam were delicious. Brad glanced at his watch, deciding that he should be reporting in to the base, whatever it might be. Bet noticed his glance.

"Jack, finish up thy tea and get Mr Brad up to Swinbeck."

Brad got up from the table thanking Bet as he did so, vowing he would try and see these kind people again if it was not too far from Swinsbeck.

He clambered into the little car again next to Jack.

"How far have we got to go now Jack?"

"Om, two mile like I would say, as the crow flies he added. That'm going by the field paths."

The two miles by the winding lanes seemed like five, until suddenly in front of them was a muddy concrete gateway with a solitary American uniformed soldier coming very drowsily out of a small hut.

He held up his hand in the usual stop signal and shone his large torch full into Jack's face.

"Where do you think you are going grandad. You can't come in here, it's restricted US property."

He shone the torch across picking up Brad's Army uniform. "Oh I am sorry 'lieutenant' I did not see you there in this special transport! I will just phone through to the officers' mess to tell them you have arrived. What name should I give?"

"Lt. Brad Slater, soldier. This is Swinsbeck I have arrived at?"

"Yes Sir, that is what they tell us this shi... mud hole is called." He picked up a shiny new field telephone, rang the bell, and after a moment, "Guardhouse here. I have a Lt. Slater reporting in. Shall I send him up in his special transport. OK." He turned back to Jack and Brad, "follow the roadway on up to the top, make a right and the officers mess is the fourth Nissan on your left. Driver, you come straight on back down here and out of my gate, we don't want you getting yourself lost in this base."

As they drove up the muddy road, to each side were the shadowy outlines of giant bulldozers and earth-moving machinery.

"I heards that they'm were doing a lot of work overs here," commented Jack wrily.

SWINSBECK

30

Brad pulled his kitbag out from the back seat of Jack's car, thanked him for the ride, turned and looked towards the Nissan hut where he could make out the shadowy doorway, hefted his bag on his shoulder and started the next phase of his life in England.

As he opened the hut door he was hit by a waft of laughter, cigarette smoke and noisy chatter. It all died away as the six men propping up the bar turned as one towards him. Only one was dressed in Army khakis, the others in dark Navy blue. The army khaki came to greet Brad, who was able to see he was a Major.

"Slater, I presume? I am Chuck Dorling and I am in command of this base and this motley collection of sailors!" He indicated the other five in navy blue.

"Brad Slater, Sir. Fresh out of the States. What's going on here with what looks like some pretty massive earth-moving machinery?"

"We are building an air-base, Sir," one of the younger-looking 'bar-proppers' replied. "I'm John Wallis, by the way. Lieutenant Junior Grade as these others don't let me forget! Here, have a beer. I seem to be in the chair, as usual!"

"Thanks, that would be just great. What are sailors doing in the middle of Devon, England, building an air-base might I ask?"

The other 'navies' introduced themselves.

"Actually we are not really sailors but SeeBees, the Navy elite engineering Corps; building this base for you guys who looks like the Airborne and your lot, the Glider Infantry, judging by your shoulder flash."

"That's enough of talk of units, John. You know we are supposed not to be giving anything away, any secrets about the base or the use it will be put to when finished. As if the locals did not know as much or more than we do! You know what they say over here: 'The walls have ears'. Come on Brad, drink up John's warm beer and we will get you settled in your quarters. We all ought to be abed as it's another day of pushing earth around and laying concrete while trying to keep five hundred GIs at work and supervise the English lorry drivers bringing in the materials. Reveille is at six, messing here at half after for coffee, Brad."

Brad woke to a dark, grey, overcast winter morning. The sounds of the base were already drowning out shouted orders as the heavy machinery was brought wheezing into life. The others were in the mess already drinking coffee with doughnuts in the other hand, when he got there.

"You best come with me today, Brad," said Chuck. "I can get you orientated on the base and find you a useful job. To be perfectly honest I am not sure why you are here yet, as I would have thought you were part of the next phase. I have not had any draft paper to say you were posted here. That is not to say that we cannot make good use of you. Here, let's go out to my Jeep for a drive around."

Brad was amazed at what met his eyes as they went out of the mess. Stretching away as far as his eye could see was a green expanse criss-crossed by wide furrows of torn brown soil, and the intervening areas pock-marked with muddy wheel marks. Here and there were piles of torn-up trees and hedges waiting to be turned into bonfires. He could not help but think what an awful rape was happening of what must previously have been small tranquil fields. It was very sad but it was all being done in the war effort so that the Allies could defeat the German aggressors. A higher authority had deemed that the destruction of this particular bit of England was necessary to achieve this objective.

Actually, he realised, the torn soil of the outer ring was in fact muddy concrete. The massive bulldozers were working with a continuous roar in the far distance, pushing the soil to each side of a hundred-foot wide new scar running straight down the length of the base through the middle of the outer ring. This, Brad decided, must be the new main runway. The nearer end was being coated with stones delivered by a constant stream of lorries and spread by four drag lines operating in tandem, like some macabre ballet, levelling and compacting the stones in several layers of decreasing size.

"Well, Brad, you can see what we are doing as our war effort," Chuck commented dryly with a wry smile, "and you can get an idea of what the layout will be. An egg-shaped ring of about a mile and a half long divided up the middle by the main drag, which is what they are working on at present." They drove on up the side for a quarter mile. "This will be the control tower; you can see they have just started on the foundations for that. Behind will be the admin., sickbay, base GI accommodation, recreation halls, shops, quartermaster's store and everything else a small town would have. About a mile away" he turned and indicated to the north "there will be another big camp built to accommodate all the GIs who will be part of the invasion force."

"What an enormous undertaking this planned invasion is. Back home nobody has any idea that all this is happening. I suppose this is actually only a small part as well," Brad commented wistfully.

"Talking of quartermasters, we had better get ourselves straight over there and fix you up with combat boots and coveralls, you are going to love the mud. There is plenty of it as you can see. It seems to cover everything and get everywhere."

"These areas that they have made, off to the side of the ring, would be bays for parking up aircraft, I expect?"

"Yes. Others will be for gun emplacements, fuel dumps, ammunition stores; you name it, everything that makes a base tick."

They drove on round the outer circle which had been completed. At the far end the ground dropped away to a wooded valley. The hazy winter sun had come out and the view over the Devon countryside was stunning, the trees in the valley pushing up through a low mist and appearing skeletal in their winter nakedness. Brad's glider pilot's eye could see that this would not be a place for an aborted take off!

"Now, what are we going to give you to do, Brad, that will be useful to you and the construction? You are not, I realise, an engineer any more than I am. I leave all that to the Navy boys, who in spite of being Navy seem pretty competent and able to read the plans! You are the second-ranking Army officer to me and we outrank them, so I suppose it's only logical that you should be my deputy."

"I must ask you one more question: When is it expected that the base will be completed and become operational? And another one. Do you know when the invasion will take place?"

"Good questions. As regards your first question: I am not sure I can give you a definite answer. The first ground was broken here, I believe, six months ago. I only came three months ago. It is now December '42. The scheduled date of finish is supposed to be the end of June next year, but whether all the ancillary work will be complete by then, we will just have to wait and see. Your second question I can't answer. In fact, it is probably only the Generals and other nobs at the top, like the President and the British Prime Minister, who have any idea. The general opinion is that nothing could possibly be ready before the autumn, and it is unlikely that it would be then with winter just round the corner. I know they have a mild climate over here in Europe, but it can be very wet and as you can see very muddy! My guess is that it will be eighteen months from now, at the earliest. Now I should really get back to my so-called office to deal with the night's defaulters that the Regulations Sergeant-Major has trolled up from the GIs in trouble with the locals. It is not a job that I enjoy. All these boys have probably never left home before and being over here is a completely new experience for them. The local dialect is quite different from what they are used to, the customs and ways of the locals can be confusing for them, so it is not surprising that they get into trouble from time to time. Some of them are only very young as well. The other thing that causes resentment is that we have everything we want. Good food, well equipped, plenty of money in comparison to the Brits, and the thing that really attracts the girls is nylon stockings! All of this upsets the local young men in particular."

"I have not seen much sign of any local inhabitants, other than the nice friendly couple who got me up here from Honiton yesterday evening. I suppose this is an agricultural area and there are not a lot of people around, anyway. I must say that I had reckoned to get some nylons for a friend!"

"Swinsbeck is only quite small. A few houses and the pub, which is where of course the trouble starts, usually over one of the local girls, some of which come up from Honiton to meet the lads. Never anything very serious, but I have got to maintain a good relationship with them. Now Christmas is only just round the corner. Work will go on here on the construction, but I want to get everybody I can away on a week's furlough. You and I had better alternate: I had planned to take the week after, so if you want to make arrangements, go ahead."

"This sounds like a good posting. Only just arrived and I am being sent off again!"

Brad thought about it that afternoon. He had only just seen Jill Pearson in London, but they had got on really well and he was very keen to meet again. He had felt sure that she had liked him and would be keen to see him again. After all, she had said come and spend some leave at the family farm; perhaps Jim would be there as well. He wrote immediately to Jill in London saying what time off he would have.

A week later, by return of post, her reply came as he had hoped. She would be down at the family home for a week over Christmas and they were expecting Jim as well, if the *Queen Mary* was obliging. Her mother and father would be very pleased if he was able to join them all, and stay as long as he wished.

Brad took the Jeep he had been allocated one afternoon and tracked down the house where Bet and Jack lived. He had the obligatory large mug of tea and left behind with them a bag of foodstuffs such as spam, peach-halves in syrup, biscuits, condensed fruit juice and other goodies he had been able to get from the base store. All things that were impossible to get in war time Britain and things that they would never have tried before. This was in the way of a thank-you for their kindness that first evening.

Christmas Eve he took the Jeep again and found his way to near Calstock, looking down the great River Tamar which ran on down to Plymouth, through the deep wooded valleys before opening out into the great expanse of the estuary, which for centuries had provided such a wonderful safe haven. Now it continued to be a haven and safe anchorage for an enormous variety of ships and boats, ranging from the biggest warships through landing-craft in enormous numbers, down to small tugs and supply ships.

He was royally received by those of the Pearson family who were at home. Jill had arrived down from London the night before. She looked quite different to Brad's eyes, dressed in her country tweed skirt and cotton blouse and out of her severe Army uniform. Her hair fell to her shoulders in soft waves and Brad was immediately even more enchanted by her. She blushed slightly as his gaze lingered on her.

"Brad, stop staring! You Americans can be so forward!" she said as she took his arm. "What are you looking at anyway?" It was now Brad's turn to colour up.

"Come and meet the rest of the family, or rather those of us who are to be here. That's Mum and Dad and Susan, my younger sister; we are expecting Jim later tonight if he is able to catch a train and the *Queen* has not been delayed. I don't think she often is as she travels so fast."

Brad had not told Jill about the tragedy he had witnessed on his trip over. Jim had been insistent that nothing should be said about it to anybody.

Mum was a homely, round, cheerful, red-cheeked person in her pinafore apron, who Brad took an instant liking to. Not a bit like Jill in her looks. Brad decided that she was a thinner version of his maternal grandmother, Mrs Barterelli. Dad, on the other hand, was willowy thin, a pencil moustache, immaculately dressed, and bow-legged (obviously a 'horsey' person by the look of him), who immediately informed Brad that he liked to be called 'Major'! He might take a little getting to know until he had realised that Brad was not just another brash American come over to steal away his 'English Rose' of a daughter. Brad realised that he would need to tread carefully until they had got to know each other better.

Jill tactfully took him by the arm, knowing full well that her father did not hesitate to speak his mind.

"Now come and let me show you the house and farm. The house dates back to mediaeval times and has been in Father's family for hundreds of years. He has lived here all his life and we are all very attached to the place. Of course he was away during the last war serving with the Devonshire Regiment and was lucky to be one of the few officers who returned after that dreadful conflict."

| THIRTY

"Say, you are a regular little history book, aren't you, with your local information and all you told me about London," he teased.

"Just because you Yanks have no history to be proud of and, anyway, although you are all from European stock, you probably have no idea about your forebears," she came straight back at him.

"I think you are quite right, actually. All I know is that my Grandfather did come from England and travelled over to the States from Liverpool, which funnily enough is where I landed."

They wandered on arm-in-arm in companionable silence for a while, enjoying the peace and tranquillity of the winter sunshine, the cooing of pigeons, and the ancient surroundings; no sound of war disturbed this perfect Christmas Eve.

Much later that evening, after an excellent dinner and Brad sharing a glass of port with the 'Major', they turned in for the night. Jill, seeing him to the door of his room, gave him a quick peck of a kiss on the cheek as she gently squeezed his arm. Half an hour later there was a knock on his door. Brad's heart missed a beat or two as he thought it was Jill returning for rather more than a kiss, though he was surprised. He hurried over and opened the door wide letting the lamp-light flood into the passage way.

"Jim... This is a surprise! I was not expecting you."

"No, I can see that by the look on your face! I think perhaps you might have hoped that it was someone else! I have only just arrived down from Plymouth on the last train. What a journey from Scotland. It is such a waste of good leave time, this travelling. Anyway, it's really good to see you here at the 'Ol' Stately Home.' I just wanted to make contact tonight; we can catch up in the morning."

Christmas week passed all too quickly with lots of good country fare, no sign of any rationing here; the three of them taking long walks through the deep snow that had arrived on Boxing Day and having cosy chats round the fire. A really well-earned relaxing time, with the strains and stresses of the last few months put aside, even if it was only temporarily. They were able to put to the back of their minds that they would have to return to it shortly. Jim tactfully left Brad and Jill some moments when they were able to get away on their own. Jim and Jill departed on the train for London, Brad back to Swinsbeck to relieve Chuck for his week's furlough. Before he left the Major took Brad aside to tell him he was more than welcome in his home at any time. Jill and he made plans to meet in London at the earliest opportunity. Their romance, though short-lived, had blossomed into something really strong and was more than just a physical attraction which would be able to survive the days and weeks of separation.

31

Swinsbeck base had progressed rapidly in Brad's absence. The main runway was half completed with the broad strip looking enormous; the control tower had sprung up to the first floor, Nissan huts had sprouted like mushrooms behind it. The whole place had begun to take on a life and feel of its own. He had the impression that the whole job was running ahead of schedule. By the end of March he was sure of this. Jill and he had met again in London for a passionate weekend and they were now planning a life together, though Brad was yet to make his proposal and, of course, had not been accepted. He was slightly dreading going to ask the Major for Jill's hand in marriage, though they now had a very good relationship.

The beginning of April saw the arrival of six PB 4Y-1 Liberator long-distance maritime aircraft; they were more generally known as B24's, these great silver four Wasp-engined planes were made in the Henry Ford factory at Detroit. They were part of the Fleet Air Wing of the 479th Air Sub-Group of the USAF. Brad, when he heard this full title, thought: why did the Army always like to have such long high-faluting names for the different arms of the services? With their flight and maintenance crews the base really began to feel operational. The officers' mess had been extended and each evening was a throbbing buzz of talk. They were young men living life to the full, which involved some serious drinking when not flying the next day. Sometimes this would involve commandeering a vehicle and visiting one of the local pubs, or a visit to Honiton.

Brad became particularly friendly with one of the pilots. In the middle of the month he negotiated, as a pilot himself, a trip on an operational patrol.

"You will just find it totally boring. Stooging out for seven hours with nothing to look at but the grey Atlantic, and then seven hours back again. I can't imagine why you would want to come. It is cold as well. If you insist, though, you can come instead of Lonnie who will be glad to miss a trip. Weather permitting, we will be off tomorrow soon after first light, about half past five. Be ready in the crew-room then for bacon and egg before we embark. We will need stoking up for the trip."

THIRTY-ONE

Brad was excited at this change from the routine he had followed on the base since his arrival, never quite sure why he was there at all.

They drove out to the Liberator aircraft, nicknamed 'The Gorgeous Belle'. This was painted on the fuselage just below the cockpit window on each side. It included a picture of a very well endowed scantily-clad young lady. Six of them: two pilots, an engineer, a radio and radar operator, a navigator and an air gunner. Brad took his seat in the co-pilot's place, donned his head-set and followed the instructions of his friend.

"OK Brad, you know the routine, hand on the throttles on mine and keep your other hand away from the control column. We have a full load of depth charges so do not want any mistakes.!"

One by one the four great engines were brought to life. The noise to Brad was indescribable, he was very glad of the flying helmet which deadened the sound slightly. He had borrowed this, along with fur-lined boots, thick padded coat and trousers, from Lonnie who he was replacing for this trip. The engines were run up to temperature and they taxied out to the end of the runway. Now Brad, from the height of the cockpit, had a different perspective of the runway from that he had been seeing every day from ground level. Although it was difficult to place exactly the runway end, his imagination told him that it could not possibly be long enough to enable this great heavy 'beast' to make the transition from the lumbering thing it was on the ground into the perfect flying machine.

Quickly they got a green Very Light from the control tower and with a surge of power they were off, accelerating fast. Brad was pushed to the back of his seat in a way that he had never experienced when flying before. The wheels came unstuck from the ground, after two-thirds of the concrete had rushed by, and were brought up into the bottom of the wings with a rumbling groan as they headed out over the wooded valley at the western end of the runway. They were soon headed out over the coast which he recognised as north-Devon from the chart spread on his knee. Then it was grey sea, after another patch of grey sea, as he had been warned. They followed a shallow zigzag course, weaving their way out, with the radar operator continually scanning the sea ahead of them for the slightest echo of a ship or submarine. They turned for home with some relief. If something were to go wrong at this point and they had to ditch in the sea there was no hope of a rescue at this distance from land. The roar of the engines now just a dull noise in their subconscious, it would be very easy to doze off, lulled by the steady drone. Brad did not often think of his father, considering the way he had neglected him, but now half-way into this long flight he wondered how he had managed to stay alert during the long flights he had made as a civil airline pilot.

Two hours later the radar operator reported excitedly several echoes way over to the port side. He thought it looked like a small convoy making its way probably back to one of the ports of the UK.

"We had better check them out. You have the day's recognition signal ready, Sparks?" The pilot enquired.

"Yes Sir, we don't want a repeat of last time when we got fired at by one of the over-eager escorts."

Brad, who had been piloting the aircraft for the last hour, turned them onto a new heading to intersect the convoy. He could feel the tension in the voices of the plane's crew increase as they drew nearer to the contact. Obviously their experience last time had had an effect on them. It must have been a dramatic change from the normal patrol boredom. Brad handed the controls back to the aircraft Captain as they swooped down through broken cloud to catch their first glimpse of the ships far below. The Radio Operator was quick to flash the identification challenge to the group of ten ships ploughing their way in two columns through what appeared to be a moderate swell. They consisted of two frigates to each side of the columns with the merchant ships tucked safely up between them. The correct recognition signal was flashed up from one of the frigates, followed by 'Thanks for looking in on us. Safe flight home and have a beer for us this evening!'

"I don't know how those chaps stick it day after day," the pilot commented. "We think our job is tedious, but they have the added worry of not knowing when a submarine has them in its sights, and they could be swimming around in the water in a couple of minutes. I guess the sea is pretty cold at this time of year too."

Another five hours of uneventful boredom and they were back doing a circuit of Swinsbeck before touching down as the light faded. It was nice to see the green of land once again. Brad was glad he had experienced the trip, but would not be keen to do it regularly. However, it was the highlight of his wartime career so far.

"Brad, come up to the office will you," Chuck asked him weeks later. "Two things I wished to talk to you about, Captain Slater. That's the first! Secondly, I have orders here for you to report to Army Headquarters at Plymouth for two days for a briefing, before returning here. Congratulations, Captain. Drinks all round the mess this evening, I think." It took a moment for Brad to realise what Chuck had said about his promotion. He wondered what difference it would actually make to him.

The extra money would come in handy, of course, although there was very little to spend it on at Swinsbeck. Brad had never been a great one for over-indulging in the pubs. The new rank would bring with it more responsibility,

| THIRTY-ONE

but he could handle that easily enough. He wondered why they wanted to see him at headquarters.

Next week he took the excuse of going to Plymouth to pay a visit to Calstock and spend a night with Major and Mrs Pearson. He was well received into the family by now so was able to have a very frank discussion with the Major about his relationship with Jill, though he was not too happy about discussing this behind her back. Brad was in love with Jill, he knew, and would like to spend the rest of his life with her as man and wife. He was pretty certain that she had the same feelings. What he was not sure about was that they were in the middle of a horrific war; at any time one or other of them could be killed. Was it the right time to be married?

He drove the jeep on to Plymouth headquarters the next morning. The briefing was about a seaborne operation to be carried out that night, 27th April, by American engineers and infantry in Tank Landing Ships at a stretch of beach called Slapton Sands in South Devon. This was a long gentle sloping shingle beach backed by a lagoon which was apparently not dissimilar to the possible landing site for the re-invasion of France, though where this would take place was not mentioned at the briefing, which everybody knew was imminent. The guess by those that thought they knew more than everybody else was the Pas de Calais, probably Dunkirk.

This was, after all, where the magnificent evacuation of thousands of troops had taken place early in the war when the Allies were pushed out after the fall of France. It would be ironic if we could go back in from where we had left. Brad was to be an observer on shore when the troops landed at Slapton for this exercise.

Midnight he drove with the other observers to await the landing expected at two in the morning. Their wait was in vain, nothing happened except for a lot of gunfire and explosions well out to sea. Eventually they heard that the operation had been aborted and returned to Headquarters.

The debriefing of the exercise revealed the appalling news that the convoy of Landing ships had been ambushed by German Motor Torpedo Boats with a great loss of American lives. It was caused by a lack of communication between the ships of the convoy, but more seriously in the planning and not allowing enough of the right sort of escorts. It was a chance unplanned attack by the Germans. They were in the habit of lying, engines stopped, on the shipping route across Lyme Bay in the hope of catching the odd coastal ship. They would hear the throb of the unsuspecting target's engines or catch a glimmer of light from a badly covered light, before dashing in under full power; torpedoes released, guns blazing and away quickly before any retaliation could be mounted.

That afternoon Brad was summoned to the commanding General's office.

"At ease, Slater, take a seat. You will be wondering why you were ordered to be an observer last night. We thought it important that the Airborne should be represented, and get an idea of the enormous operation that needs to be mounted. You will play a small part in that operation, but an important part none the less. Now I wish to put you in the picture as regards the role which Swinsbeck and your team will play in the forthcoming invasion. I am sure you have been wondering why you were posted to Swinsbeck. The airfield was not built solely for the Maritime Reconnaissance Liberators. Very shortly you will be getting a draft of Waco CG-4A gliders, or it may be a mix of these and the British Horsa glider. At the moment I am not sure what is available, you will just have to see what turns up; they will be brought in by C-47 DC3 Dakotas. Your orders are to take command of this unit. Train them up and prepare for when they are needed. Not even I have knowledge of when that will be. You will be familiar with the Dakota, but your training in California could have been on the Horsa glider, am I not right? Good luck."

32

Sure to the General's word, two days later six Dakotas circled over Swinsbeck, each with a single glider following close behind. The roar of the Dakotas brought everybody out to gaze at these intruders into the airspace that had previously belonged only to the Liberators and the occasional B17 bomber, returning from a raid on the industrial cities of Germany and damaged by anti-aircraft fire or night fighter planes. The gliders looked like giant dragonflies, with their bulbous noses. The tug-planes were cut loose by the gliders leaving the umbilical chord of the tow rope trailing behind each Dakota. Almost silently, except for a soft swishing noise, one by one, they swooped in to land on the grass verge of the runway. Some landing with hardly a bump; others hopping down the grass, but all making it safely to a stop. Brad felt he had been holding his breath to get them all down in one piece. These were after all the tools of his new team. All these six were the American-built Waco. Though far from an experienced glider pilot himself, he had made a lot of landings with powered aircraft. He could not but help feeling admiration for the pilots who were landing these unpowered aircraft; they had only the one chance to 'hit' the right spot. Once the gliders were all safely down and the runway was clear, the Dakotas came into circuit and were able to drop down to land, taxiing straight into the holding bays round the base circuit road. Tow tractors rushed out to the gliders to drag them away to the dispersals to be carefully camouflaged with netting. It had been impressed on Brad that the base was to look like an operational Liberator base to any casual German plane that managed to make it through the RAF's tight protective screen. The big silver planes would draw the eye rather than well-hidden gliders which would have given away the true purpose of the base as a stage for the forthcoming invasion.

Brad went out to meet the new arrivals. He was really surprised to find that of the six pilots, three were young women. They were all only ferry crew bringing the planes from the assembly base in the Midlands. They were to return by light aircraft later in the day, ready to bring in the next batch, until he thought there were to be thirty gliders under his command. The pilots for his command would be arriving the next day. It was four years since Brad had done his glider training and he couldn't help wondering whether this new batch of trainees, straight out of the glider course, would be more competent than himself. During those four years he had done the odd flight in a light powered aircraft, but had not even set eyes on a glider. However, his job was to take command of the little group, not to teach them how to fly.

Sure enough, as the next lot of Dakotas came to a standstill, having watched their charges safely land, they spewed out a diverse mix of men of various rank, size, colour and all full of young American brashness and confidence. Brad went out with the truck to collect them. The next day, as they gathered with Brad in a mess hall, he realised that he was going to have his hands full to get these rookies into the state of mind and ability to be able to land a glider for the one important occasion that was required on the appointed day. Half of them had never flown before arriving at the training base, let alone been pilots. His initial feeling was one of anger that he should have been sent what could be just the dregs of the Army. He soon realised that this was not so, in fact they were all volunteers; intelligent young men who wished to be doing something special with a bit of action rather than being drafted as a bog-standard GI. They had all come from Lubbock, Texas, after initial GI training. There were a couple who had flown light aircraft before the war, which was an asset. Brad divided the rest into two platoons under the command of these qualified pilots. He made a field appointment by giving them the rank of Flight Officer.

The first thing was to get them familiar with the cockpit layout and the glider generally before they started flying. Brad decided the best thing was to start off in the base briefing room, to remind them all of the capabilities and specifications of the two types of glider.

He really felt quite nervous about standing up in front of these 'confident' young men.

"You may smoke." he started off. "I just thought we would have a brief session in here to familiarise ourselves with the two types of toys we have been provided with. I suspect that you have all seen a Waco glider. Has anybody come across the British Horsa? No, well let me start with that and compare the two. We may get some of them in the next few days. It is about half as big again as the Waco, although its wingspan is much the same. It can carry 28 men, as against 13 for the Waco, plus their equipment or a mix of men and light vehicles. Both are made primarily of wood with a painted fabric covering. The Horsa has the capability of jettisoning its tricycle undercarriage after take off and landing on a skid. Any of you that do that during training here will be put on a charge!" he tried to liven his talk up with this poor joke, but it received only a

| THIRTY-TWO

polite 'snort' from his bored-looking audience, many lounging with their feet over the chair in front of them, caps tipped well back on their heads. "Towing speed is about 150 mph, or whatever the tug is able to make if the wind is against it. If the speed drops to under 50 mph then you will stall and fall out of the sky! Landing speed should be about 60 mph. This will give you a sinking drop of 400 feet per minute. If you cut loose from the tug too early then you won't be able to reach the landing area. Both types need about 200-250 yards in which to land. We will train here, until we are needed, on a much bigger space so I will have marked out on the grass this distance and we will keep at it until we can hit this target every time. Well that's all I want to say for now, so we had better get out there and see what we have got. Any questions at this stage?"

"Yes Sir. When will we be going. I have been here for less than twenty four hours and already I am wondering what we are going to do in this out-of-the-way place. I am a city boy from San Francisco and am being driven nuts by the quiet."

"Well soldier, I think I can guarantee that we will keep you busy. We all have a lot to learn, and it is a matter of life and death that we get it right for 'on the day'. Not only our own lives, but don't forget that you will be carrying passengers with their lives depending upon your skill. As regards when will we be going. I have no idea when or where it will be. Just be thankful that it probably will not be for several months. Enjoy the peace while you can, it won't be pleasant when we do go."

They trooped out to one of the gliders.

At the front of the box-like body was a bulbous nose, with its large all-round windscreen, which was where any big equipment was loaded. The whole front hinged up to make a large opening, there were also access doors on each side of the fuselage. The cockpit contained two seats, each with a control yoke in front of it. The yokes were connected by wires to the minimal control surfaces of the glider, rudder for small adjustments of direction, wing flaps for the balance of the glide and to flare out at touch-down, as well as for sharper turns. Between the yokes were a minimum of altitude and speed instruments, and the all-important release handle for cutting free from the tug. A very basic layout designed to serve one purpose only for a one off occasion, namely to enable the pilot to put the glider down on a particular spot. This was a 'throw away' machine that would not be used for a second time.

These young men were full of over-confidence which Brad knew would very quickly disappear as they became airborne and the sheer horror of getting themselves back to earth, in the right place, sank in.

They all worked hard through the summer months, progressing as best as possible through the theory again and again of making a safe landing and flight in general, until Brad deemed they were ready for the real thing. The idea was that the glider would leave the ground shortly before the tug. It would follow straight behind the tow attached to it by the tow line fixed to the glider on the wing stubs each side of the body. The glider would continue to fly just above the Dakota's flight path to try and avoid some of the turbulence from the Dakotas Pratt and Whitney radial engines.

A Dakota was made available for their use and one by one they took to the air, each accompanied by either Brad or one of the Flight Officers in the co-pilot's seat. All went well, apart from the odd small accident when the glider tipped on its nose. Not an uncommon occurrence. No great damage was done to either man or machine, although there were inevitably some 'exciting' moments.

Tow speed was supposed to be 150 mph and this dropped to a very maximum of 100 mph as they came in to land after one circuit of Swinsbeck. It was with considerable relief when they had all had a flight and were able to go and brag about it all in their respective messes at the end of the day. Brad was under no illusion that when the real thing came it would be quite different, landing under fire. As autumn drew into winter, training became intermittent due to the weather. If they could not fly he had them in the briefing room covering the theory, once again, or out doing maintenance on the gliders. He worked them hard but also expected them to play hard.

33

Christmas was once again spent at Calstock with Jill and her parents. Jim was not there this year, he was somewhere on the high seas. Christmas Eve was Brad's crowning day when he asked Jill to be his wife and she accepted. They felt that they could not wait for the war to be over, it could drag on for several more years. It would be silly to delay any longer. They were in love and 'minor' details like the war could be forgotten very easily, even if only for the day. The Major, thankfully for Brad, when asked if he approved, also accepted Brad to be his son-in-law and gave the union every blessing. He disappeared down the cellar coming up a few minutes later with a crusty old bottle of champagne, which had probably lain there since The Major had inherited the house.

Over Christmas they made plans for the ceremony. The idea was that the wedding would be a quiet affair with just a few family and friends. Brad was sort of sorry that his father would not be able to be with him on that special day, but he had taken so little interest in Brad's early years and upbringing that he did not deserve to even be told. He was really Brad's only close relative. He would much rather have been able to have his 'aunt' Patience, his mother's sister, and Mrs Barterelli both of whom had brought him up after his mother died.

The date of the wedding could not be fixed, as they planned it should be the first time that Jim could be with them to act as Brad's best man. This turned out to be the first weekend in April, a bright sunny spring day but with a cold north-easterly wind blowing down off Dartmoor. The cherry blossom was just starting to come out. The hedgerow banks covered in primroses, celandines, and dandelions. In the woods the carpet of bluebells was beginning to turn a hazy blue. As Jill came down the aisle Brad's heart nearly burst at the thought that this exquisite woman was in a few minutes to become his wife. He counted himself so lucky, and it had only come about by the chance meeting with Jim on the *Queen*. Chuck was the only other American at the ceremony in the little church at Calstock.

Jill had managed to have herself transferred from London to a similar post in Plymouth and after a weekend's honeymoon at the remote Dartmeet Hotel they returned to their respective jobs. Invasion fever was in the air and Brad stepped up the training of his small group. They were now all under no illusion of what was in store for them.

It soon became apparent that Jill was pregnant and she gave up her job to be with Brad.

Early in May he took the tenancy of the farm whose land had been commandeered for building the base. Up to this time they had been living in a small rented house in Honiton which, because of both of their jobs, they were only able to make use of when their off-duty days coincided. The farmhouse was rather run-down as ever since the land had been compulsorily purchased by the government two years before, the house had stood empty. It was damp and cold inside when they moved in, but it had quickly warmed up once they had a good fire going in the living room, with its enormous fireplace and chimney which still had the bars and hooks for hanging hams to cure in the wood smoke. The old black range in the kitchen gave the same result The thick walls of the house acted like a hot brick once they were warmed through. They had quickly fallen in love with its cob walls and slated roof, and particularly the homely feel it all had about it.

At least it had running water and electricity, both supplied by a generator. They had, of course, no use for the old cow stalls, big tithe barn and pig pens across the cobbled yard. It had for them both, and especially Brad, a rather special feel to it. Cogwell Barton Farm, with its big beech trees sheltering it, felt like it had been home for ever.

Mid-May the training had reached its peak. Brad felt confident that each of his pilots was on top form. He just hoped that the invasion would be very soon. They were beginning to be 'over-trained', which resulted in some unnecessary mishaps, though none serious. As he put it to them: 'You could put a handkerchief down with a dime on it. You could then put one of the glider wheels down on the dime. That's how well I feel you can handle these aircraft.'

He was called to Plymouth on the 31st May for a meeting, which proved to be his orders for his little group's part in the landing, the date of which was still not being divulged, even if it was known. It was interesting as he was able to see a mock-up model cleverly made of sand and cloth of the landing area, though there was no indication to which part of Europe it applied. It showed a stretch of coastline very similar to where the disastrous exercise of two months previously had been meant to take place. Behind the coast was a body of water with a few causeways across it, leading to rising ground covered in a mass of small hedged fields. The landing area was inland from this, but worried Brad as it looked far too small to take his gliders safely. They would need to touch down as soon as possible by skimming the hedge.

All personnel were confined to base. This had to be an indication that 'D-day', as it was designated, was very imminent.

During the last few months the new camp up the road from Swinsbeck had filled up with hundreds of GIs who were destined to make the landing either from ships and amphibious craft or by parachute, in which case they would be taking off from Swinsbeck.

Loading of the gliders with field guns, jeeps or light tanks was to begin the next day. The orders were that the gliders would go in the day after the planned landing, to reinforce the paratroops who would have secured the ground behind the landing beach designated Utah. The sand/cloth model had been brought up from Plymouth and placed in the briefing room under a secure cover. It would only be revealed to Brad's team the day before they were to fly. They could then familiarise themselves with the terrain around their touchdown area. This was pretty vital so that they could identify certain landmarks and know that they needed to be at a particular height as they crossed that position to give them the accurate landing they needed.

In addition to the 'hardware' each glider would be carrying up to 25 men of the 325th Glider Infantry, the number depending on the weight of the 'hardware'

34

The beginning of June came in with rain and gales making an invasion out of the question both for the seaborne forces and airborne gliders and paratroops. The planned invasion had to be cancelled temporarily which meant troops being held in the tented camps in poor overcrowded conditions, which inevitably lead to many additional problems. Then quite suddenly, on the 5th, Brad's Dakotas were all commandeered to take part in the great landing and drop, which was scheduled for the next day. All hands were put to work hastily before the Dakotas were loaded with paratroops, to paint three white identification bands on the tail and round the wing stubs of each aircraft. Each of the gliders was marked in a similar fashion. A weather window had suddenly been forecast by the Meteorological Officers. The troop passengers arrived to bivouac on the base margins. Late that night they began embarking in the aircraft. Brad walked over to chat with them as they rested on the grass. The sky was quite cloudy with odd glimpses of the full moon shining through the scudding clouds.

"You make sure you look after my planes!" he joked with them. "I need them back all in one piece for us to use in 24 hours!"

At this late stage they still had no idea where they were going to be dropped, but presumably the pilots had been given the route they had to follow to reach the drop zone. Each platoon officer had his sealed orders giving him his objectives once they were on the ground.

Brad was thankful that he was not going to jump out of an aeroplane. Each soldier seemed to be overloaded with his parachute, weapon, rations, ammunition and other kit. How they would not just plummet to earth with all that weight, he could not think. They had to be helped to climb the short length of steps into the plane.

Shortly after midnight the tranquil peace of the night was shattered as the Dakotas ran up their engines prior to take off. Then one by one they followed each other round the ring path onto the end of the runway before, with a burst of power, rolling off and staggering up into the night sky. The invasion had started. These would be the first Allied troops to land in the early hours of the morning.

The next morning the Dakotas were back, some looking a little the worse for wear with bullet holes or shrapnel damage, but all serviceable for their towing job. The ground maintenance teams went to work as soon as the planes stopped to make the necessary repairs and patching up. The pilots were full of their experiences and excitements, all still full of the adrenalin rush they had had to keep them going. The weather over the drop zone had not been particularly good and the anti-aircraft fire had made navigation and keeping on the right route rather difficult. Reports of a great invasion came with them. They had gone in with the paratroops soon after midnight to drop behind the coast. As they came out they could see, by the flashes of moonlight through the clouds, the enormous armada of ships of all sizes and descriptions heading in towards the Normandy coast. The invasion had not happened at the Pas de Calais as the know-alls had predicted.

The glider passengers loaded at midnight that evening. They sat down each side of the fuselage, with the jeeps, guns, etc. down the middle between them. Brad took his place up front at the controls and the glider - named Apple One - was pulled into place behind its tug Dakota, the 350-foot nylon tow rope attached and they were ready to go. They seemed to be kept waiting for ages. Brad was in radio contact with the control tower and gathered that the delay was due to the amount of air traffic round the invasion beaches.

Behind Brad, in the lead, was a staggered row of the other gliders stretching out onto the taxi-way, each with its tug-Dakota gently ticking over as they waited for the green light to give them permission to go. Looking round down the length of the fuselage Brad could see his 'passengers' in the dim light. Most were sitting quietly, deep in their own thoughts, some had a poker school going, many puffing away nervously on cigarettes or checking over their equipment for the umpteenth time; but all like Brad just wanting to get on with the job. At least he had something to do during the flight, they could only sit and wait. Last minute air reconnaissance of their landing site had shown what looked like obstacles, but they would have to see when they got there. He put it out of his mind for the time being, there were other more important things to think about.

It was much more difficult to put Jill out of his mind. His love for her, if it were possible, had grown and grown as their child had developed in her rapidly extending stomach. Brad had reluctantly said his goodbyes to Jill at the farm two days before. It had been difficult leaving her so sad and crying. He had assured her he should be home again within days if all went well, but now he had to be entirely focused on the task confronting him. This is what he and his little force had trained so hard for, the nervous tension continued through the whole plane. Nobody knew what the next hours would bring. The GIs were all so far from home. The law of averages said that some of them would not be returning home ever. Some would return wounded or mentally scarred by the experience they were about to participate in.

The green light, signalling them to go, flashed out from the control tower and the early morning light strengthened as the rising sun briefly peeped out from the clouds hanging over the horizon. This was it, there was no going back now. Brad could hear the sudden engine revving noise increase from the tug ahead of them and with a jerk the nylon rope taughtened as it took up the slack and they were on the move.

Quickly he got the glider airborne and the tug-Dakota eventually rose from the ground in front of him. His full concentration was on placing his aircraft steadily behind but slightly above the tug and keeping it as steady as possible in the light wind blowing across them. Sound was muted, just the faint hum from in front and dead silence from inside the glider. He was unable to see what was happening behind, but could picture the other 29 gliders rising in formation, one by one. In each one there were similar men, all having the same feelings of apprehension about what lay ahead. He caught a quick glimpse of Cogwell Farm to his right, bathed in a shaft of bright sunlight. He could picture his dear Jill tucked up safely in bed, or more likely the engine noise would have roused her and she would be watching from the window. The end of the runway fell away behind them as they ascended over the wooded valley filled with a blanket of mist. Then as they gained height the definition of fields and house became more blurred.

The Devon countryside gave way to the steely waters of the English Channel; even now a mass of shipping was plying in both directions as more troops and supplies were delivered constantly to the fragile beach head. Reports overnight had been optimistic that the landing had in the main gone well with no more than the expected casualties. What was rather more of a worry to Brad was that he had heard that many of the paratroops had been dropped away from their designated areas and some of the targets had not been secured. However, news was sketchy and probably inaccurate. The way 'gossip' became exaggerated it was more than likely not correct. Their landing area was supposed to have been taken by some of the paratroops Brad had seen off two nights before; they were going in to relieve them. The French coast came in sight. It all looked so quiet and peaceful from this height as they were crossing to the west of the invasion area. This did not last for long as they were met by an anti-aircraft barrage, the tracer shells seeming to creep lazily up the sky towards them, with the black bursts of the shells dotting the sky round them. A radio message came back to Brad from his tug that they were approaching his release point. He just hoped that the navigator up front had got it right and had not been put off by the gunfire. His heart missed several beats as he realised he was unable to see any familiar landmarks that he had memorised from the sand model. Should he trip the tow rope or stay hooked up to the tug and wait? If he waited what would be the reaction of the tug? There was not much they could do about it other than drag him all the way back to England where he would probably be court-martialled. As these thoughts rushed through his head his co-pilot pointed down to their left.

"There, Skipper. That church spire looks very like the one on the model at St.Lo. I am sure of it."

"Yes, thank God, I think you are right. I was beginning to get worried" Brad admitted. "OK, I have the release signal now, so all is well. Pull the leaver and let's join the war. Keep looking out for the landing field, Joe. Give the bodies behind us that we are five minutes away from landing. You can give them a final warning to brace themselves just before we go in. OK, here we go."

He had got his bearings now and turned them onto the heading to take them in. The other gliders behind them would be partially relying on him to get it right, they were really like a lot of sheep.

He could just make out the sea away to his left with the lagoon of marshy water behind the low beach of sand dunes dotted with the signs of war. Landing craft at unusual angles to the beach, a smattering of vehicles, the dots of men. The causeways across the lagoon, narrow strips of raised ground through the water littered with Jeeps, tanks and still bodies. The fighting had obviously been heavy to gain the hard ground, which was pock-marked with craters from shell fire and mortars. At the land end the craters and torn earth was even greater where the bombardment from the off-lying warships, before the landing, had ripped the ground apart.

35

The gliders' landing site was meant to be about two miles inland from the beach-head on level fields, which should have been taken in the last twenty-four hours by the initial assault paratroops. As Brad turned into his final approach he was able to see several of the other gliders following on behind him, sweeping majestically down. He hoped they had all made it through the anti-aircraft barrage, or come to that there had not been any accidents on take-off. Take-off and landing were the two critical times for flying. Once you were up there it was pretty straight forward and safe.

His co-pilot, Joe, had sharper, younger eyes than Brad, apart from which he did not have to control the glider and so was free to look around and pick out their reference points.

"I've got it. You are smack on track. Oh, my God, there appear to be things in the field. It looks bloody small too. I suppose that really is our site. Everything round it fits with the model, so it must be."

Brad could see the designated landing area now. Joe was right, it did look as if there were obstructions. It looked like a whole lot of posts driven into the ground. He wondered if the nearby fields would be possible, but realised quickly that they all looked a lot smaller so were quite out of the question. This was why this field had been selected, and why the Germans had filled it with obstacles, being the only possible field around that was a suitable glider landing area.

Then his full concentration was taken by the landing. As he dropped down through 500 feet he was met by withering machine-gun fire rising up from the far end of the field beyond. They had not been expecting that. They had thought that the paratroops would have cleared the area by now so that they could make an unopposed landing. This was going to make the unloading of the gliders very difficult. They would be stuck out in the open in the middle of the field; there were going to be casualties. He wondered if he could manage to get the glider to stop up against the far hedge; with the bank as well it would then give them some protection. The trouble with that idea was that he had no control over the glider once it was on the ground. If this was not bad enough he could see, spaced regularly across the field, that the posts they had seen from above were in fact made of metal-designed to cause as much damage to the gliders as possible.

Time seemed to stand still as the machine-gun fire criss-crossed in front of the cockpit canopy, finally finding the range and shattering the Perspex windscreen into a thousand pieces. The whole lot imploded inwards and Brad once again had a clear view as they dived towards the ground. A warm sticky liquid ran down his left cheek from just below his helmet. There was no pain, but as he brushed his gloved hand across it he realised that a bit of Perspex from the windscreen must have nicked him. He could hear agonised screams coming from behind him. Some poor bugger has caught it, he thought. He glanced sideways towards Joe who was slumped in his harness; with horror Brad could see that his whole face was completely shattered by a direct hit. At the same time his left leg erupted in a sea of pain as he received a hit. He pointed the glider in his semi-conscious state at a gap between the metal posts, only to realise that these were what they knew as "Hitler's Asparagus." Each post was linked to its neighbours' by a wire which triggered off a Teller mine on each post.

They were very nearly down, he had achieved his objective, the job was done. Nothing could stop them now.

In spite of his wound he made what he thought was a copybook landing, hoping in a fleeting moment that the following pilots would have noticed! He managed to miss the posts but as Apple-One ran between them the mines neatly amputated the wings showering shrapnel into the fuselage, causing horrible wounds amongst the troops lining each side. They came to a shuddering halt, skewed at an angle, but only about twenty yards off the hedge bank. They would have little protection. Other gliders came in to each side of them, some managing to miss the post as Brad had achieved, others having dreadful accidents as they were impaled on the posts and the mines exploded. The remaining GIs in Brad's glider scrambled to get their equipment out and to engage the machine-guns causing such havoc. Brad could only stay sitting in his seat, his leg shattered. As he drifted in and out of the relief of unconsciousness he thought that this wound would keep him out of the war for a few weeks. He could hear the bullets 'zipping' through the glider's skin with the odd metallic 'zing' as one hit metal. Then he was punched hard in the chest by another hit. He felt no pain but seemed to drift into a lovely peaceful state of hazy blue skies and green trees. He was with Jill and between them, each holding one of his hands was a little boy. They were all laughing happily as they walked in the sunshine. His head dropped slowly onto his chest as life left him…

EPILOGUE

Eleven months and two days after June 6th the bloody battle to restore peace in Europe finally succeeded.

Thankfully, future generations of Slaters, and everybody else, have been able to enjoy that peace which was so bravely won. Horrific wars have continued 'locally' throughout the world from time to time, but hopefully the human race has learnt that never again can they experience the slaughter of two Great Wars.

Brad did not live to see his son born to his widow, Jill, nine months to the day after their marriage in the ancient church at Calstock in rural Devon. The boy entered the world without fuss where the Slaters had all arrived from time immemorial: the front bedroom of Cogwell Barton.

Once again, after eighty-four years, a Slater boy had returned who would be able to carry the name forward.

As they had for centuries, seeing so much history, and would continue to do so forever more.

The southwest wind gusted in with a 'gentle' edge to it, rocking the branches of the big beech trees, but this early in the autumn, as yet unable to blow the leaves away in a cloud of gold, as it would achieve in about a month's time.

The Slaters were hanging on at Cogwell Barton.

BIOGRAPHY

David Barrow was born in Surrey in 1935. After completing his education at Charterhouse and serving in the Royal Navy, he trained in agriculture, before eventually acquiring a farm in Dorset. After thirty years farming there, he and his family moved to Devon where he ran a tree nursery, before "retirement" and a new career as a writer. This is his second novel.

Also by the author

Flight of a Habit

The tale is told by Cris, an ex public schoolboy, with inherited money, recently thrown out of the Army having had a spell in detention for selling MOD property. He meets Coleen, a prostitute, only in the game to improve her prospects by making quick money. She is of Irish/Columbian extraction with family still living in Columbia.

The two of them decide to visit Columbia and Colleen's family, where they are welcomed. While on an expedition in the jungle they are kidnapped by guerrillas and discover that the Columbian family are in the cocaine exporting business.

Looking for more adventure they decide to try their hand at smuggling cocaine into England. The story unfolds as they plan and execute the operation through Portugal, Spain, France, and finally England where it reaches a dramatic conclusion in the Devon countryside.

This is an enthralling adventure story. Once started it is difficult to put down.

Obtainable from all good bookshops or from 01884 266155. £8 inc. p&p.